GLASS
HANDBOOKS

Lamination

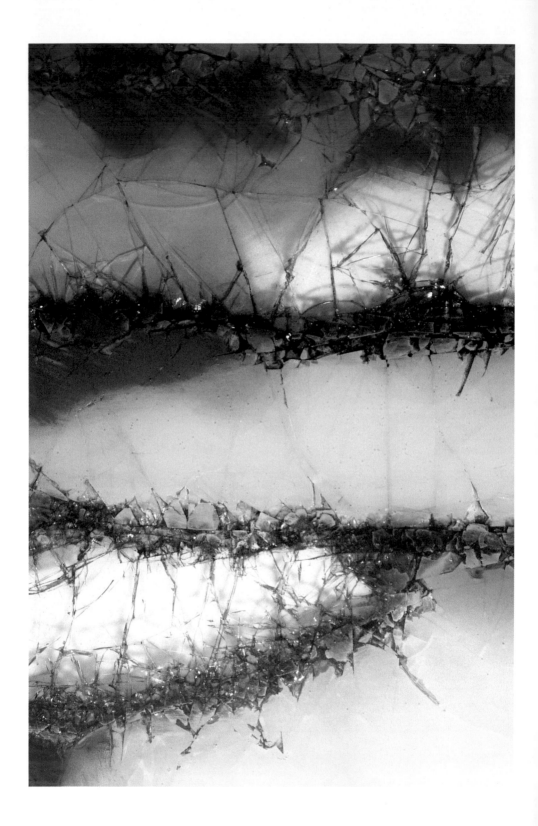

GLASS
HANDBOOKS

Lamination

GEORGE PAPADOPOULOS

A & C Black • London

First published in Great Britain in 2004
A & C Black Publishers Limited
Alderman House, 36 Soho Square
London W1D 3QY
www.acblack.com

ISBN 978-0-7136-6163-7

Reprinted 2011

CIP Catalogue records for this book are
available from the British Library and the
U.S. Library of Congress.

Book design by Susan McIntyre
Cover design by Dorothy Moir
Copyedited by Rebecca Harman
Proofread by Paige Weber
Typeset in 10 on 13pt Photina

Printed and bound by Star Standard PTE.,
Ltd, Singapore

A & C Black uses paper produced with el-
emental chlorine-free pulp, harvested from
managed sustainable forests.

CONTENTS

PREFACE

When I was approached by A&C Black to write a book on glass lamination, I was reluctant to take it on, partly because of the amount of work involved, and partly because English is not my first language. Like most artists, though, I was also suspicious of telling people about the processes and techniques I'd evolved in my studio. So writing this book has been liberating for me on two counts. First, it has made me look back over my own practice, and see where it has come from and where it might go. Second, it has made me realise that making art is not a competitive business: it is a process of collaboration. I hope that readers will take whatever they can from my own experience, and from the discoveries of the other artists and professionals mentioned in this book.

ACKNOWLEDGEMENTS

I would like to thank my family for their unfailing support, and especially my sister, Maria Whalley, who kept me sane and fed in lean times. Sean O'Mahony has been the kind of assistant I hope you will all have the luck to find, and a brilliant friend and adviser to boot. Jim Langlands has kept me supplied with resin, and Barbara Derix and her family with inspiration, support and meat-balls; the Crafts Council has also been unfailingly supportive. Philippa and Ian Fraser kindly lent me their house in Majorca to write this book, which I started and finished at the Mount Pleasant writers' retreat in Surrey; and Richard Jackson introduced me to the world of laminating and to A&C Black. Finally, I would like to thank my friend, Charles Darwent, without whom this book would (literally) not have been possible.

Introduction

Some time in 1909, a French chemist called Edouard Benedictus knocked a glass flask off a high shelf on to the floor of his laboratory in Paris. Although the fall was from a height of 3 m, the flask did not smash. When Benedictus examined it, he found that it was completely shattered but had held together. Some interior bond, invisible but strong, had kept the glass from splintering.

Checking his records, Benedictus saw that he had last used the flask 15 years before, and that it had then contained a mixture of alcohol, ether, acetone, amyl acetate and trinitrocellulose. The mixture had evaporated over time, and it was the residue from this evaporation that had coated the inside of the flask. The resulting compound was completely transparent, behaved like celluloid and was very durable. It was this that had held the broken flask together.

As is the way with great discoveries, Benedictus wrote down his findings, threw the flask away and immediately forgot about it. It was six years later, reading the report of a traffic accident in Paris in which two young women had been badly cut by glass from a shattered windscreen, that it struck the chemist that his transparent compound might have a practical use. He took two sheets of regular windscreen glass and sandwiched them together with a layer of his mysterious resin between them. Like the flask in his laboratory, the resultant product turned out to hold together even when it was shattered with a hammer.

Benedictus quickly patented his process and set up a company to manufacture his bonded glass – which, being in three layers, he called 'Triplex' – on a commercial basis. Among the first clients of the Société du Verre Triplex was the ballerina Anna Pavlova, who realised the threat that a scarred face would mean to her career. By 1912, the Triplex Safety Glass Company had opened an office in London, although laminated glass remained a fairly small business until an American auto manufacturer was nastily cut in a car accident in 1927. That manufacturer's name was Henry Ford and the rest, as they say, is history.

OPPOSITE: *How lamination began*

My own laminating history

The story of glass lamination begins with a series of accidents: Benedictus dropping his flask, two French women crashing their car and Henry Ford skidding on a dark road. My introduction to laminated glass as an art material came about in a similar way.

In 1997, I began an MA course in Ceramics and Glass at the Royal College of Art in London. From the start, I was not a good student. Glass tends to be treated with huge respect by artists and craftsmen, as a medium which is fragile and hard to work with. Breakage in the glass world is not seen as a good thing.

When my early experiments with kiln forming went wrong – my impatient breaking of the rules when cooling molten glass led to a lot of breakages – my tutors were not particularly happy. I, on the other hand, was delighted. As a budding ceramicist, I had always loved *craquelure*, the crackling in glazed surfaces. The more broken the results of my kiln forming, the happier I was. And this happiness reached a peak when I accidentally dropped a sheet of glass on the studio floor one day and, just like Benedictus, was amazed to see that it had broken but not shattered.

My first sheet of broken glass, with blue light behind

My first sheet of broken glass, with green light behind

Unbeknown to me, the glass in question was laminated; it had not just broken, but broken beautifully. Like Benedictus, I too forgot about my discovery until I started on a work placement at a commercial glass studio in London that summer.

Fusion Glass was already making a product, Shattered Laminate, that used breakage to produce decorative results. In this process, a sheet of toughened glass was laminated between two sheets of float glass using a polyester-based resin. When a corner of the toughened sheet was tapped with the point of a hammer, the sheet shattered but – being in a resin sandwich – held together. I was struck by the implications of this for my beautiful broken sheet back in the glass studio at the Royal College. For the rest of the summer, I spent my free time breaking laminated glass and then re-laminating it between layers of float glass and resin.

Five years later, I am still breaking glass and putting it back together. I am often asked what this process is called: people are fond of describing it as 'a contemporary take on stained glass' although, of course, it is not. Over the past five years, I have broken glass with hammers, bricks, bullets and electrical currents. I have worked on glass that has been broken for me by a bag full of lead shot intended to replicate the exact impact of a standard human body running into a standard window. I have treated this broken glass with crayons, pastels, gold leaf, pencils, car enamels, oils, commercial spray paints and just about anything else that has come to hand in my studio (including, frequently – though accidentally – drops of my own blood). I still do not know what the process is called and, frankly, I do not care. What I do know is that laminated glass is an enormously exciting material to work with, and that my experiments with it are just beginning. That is why I am writing this book.

THOMAS

Although this book is primarily about making your own laminates, a number of artists also exploit the visual effects that can be achieved by using the different kinds of industrially laminated glass in different ways. The point about all of these pre-made glasses is that they hold together when they are broken: hit them with a hammer, and they will shatter but stay in one piece. The same is true, only more dramatically so, of bulletproof glass. Shoot sheets of it with a high-velocity rifle and those sheets will merely craze,

Thomas and his gun

attractively, around the point of impact. This odd ambiguity of things staying together while breaking apart, of violence converted into beauty,

is something that has long appealed to the Paris-based artist, Thomas. Thomas was one of the first artists to recognise the potential of laminated glass in making artworks. He shoots panels of bullet-proof glass and decorates them with pigments (and sometimes other materials such as gold leaf) to produce images that look oddly like flower-paintings. More recently, he has made sculptures that he has shown at the bottom of a swimming pool, requiring would-be visitors to view them through diver's masks.

'Comète', Thomas

'Temps d'un pacte', Thomas

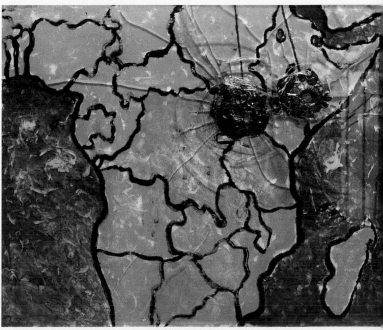

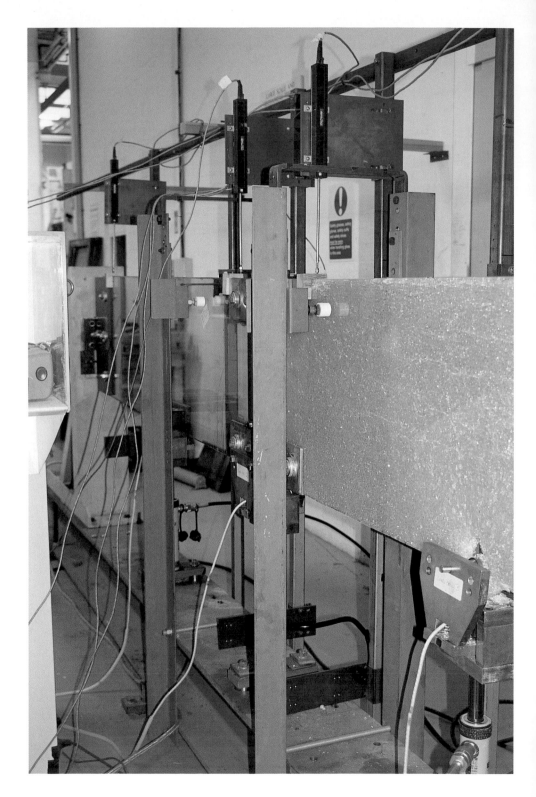

Industrial glass and the industrial aesthetic

Pilkington plc

Pilkington plc is the world's largest manufacturer of glass. In 1971, the company bought the Triplex name. Today, Pilkington is at the front end of research into glass lamination, which makes it an interesting place for a would-be glass artist to visit.

The vast majority of Pilkington's laminated glass is made for two international markets, namely the automotive industry and the building trade. Obviously, this means that most of the company's glass is made using mass production methods. In these, a thin film of polyvinylbutyral (PVB) resin is applied to a bottom layer of glass, to which a top layer is added using high-pressure (or 'nip') rollers. The resultant laminate sandwich is heat-sealed under low pressure conditions in an autoclave, a kind of massive electric pressure cooker.

As most artists' studios are unlikely to contain large machines of this kind, the practical applications of Pilkington's production methods to artists are few and far between. Whether you choose to use pre-laminated glass, laminate your glass

Pilkington plc's laminating test laboratory

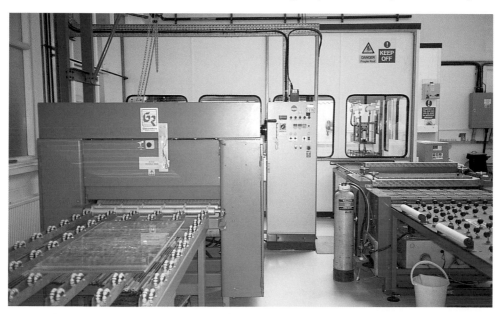

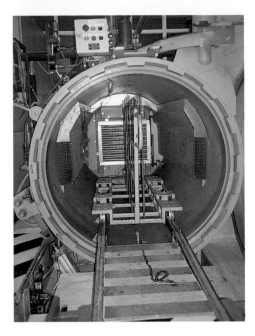

The autoclave at Pilkington's research and development centre, St Helens

Pilkington's Human Impact Resistance Test

yourself or do a combination of both, you will be working with a process that is essentially industrial. For many artists, this will add to lamination's charms: after all, the industrial aesthetic – machines, mass production, warehouse galleries, art factories – has been one of the most important influences on the art of the past 100 years. Finding beauty in a material designed for use in car wind-screens or the outer skin of skyscrapers has a special fascination of its own.

You can see this at Pilkington's research and development centre near St Helens in northwest England. There, sci-entists like Dr John Evason (Pilkington's head of glass forming and one of the world's leading experts on laminates) do terrible things to glass: exposing it to intense light and extremes of cold and heat, and simulating the various acci-dents which laminated glass is made to

withstand. In one test, ex-frozen chickens are fired at aviation glass at speeds of up to 300 mph to see how well the panels stand up to the bird-strikes to which aeroplane windscreens are prone. This once famously led to yet another level of glass accident, when technicians at Pilkington's Japanese subsidiary forgot to defrost the chickens before firing them.

For the artist, all this can only count as inspiration. As I write, I am working on a set of panels left over from Pilkington's Human Impact Resistance Test (HIRT), a procedure in which a leather bag full of lead shot is swung at sheets of laminated glass in order to recreate the exact blow of a human body running into a window. Like any work involving laminated glass, the HIRT panels combine control with accident, industrial grit with aesthetic delicacy; and, like any such work, they are utterly fascinating.

'Impact 3' (2003), Yorgos Studio

ABOVE: 'Impact 1' (2003), detail, Yorgos Studio BELOW: 'Impact 1, 2, 3' (2003), Yorgos Studio

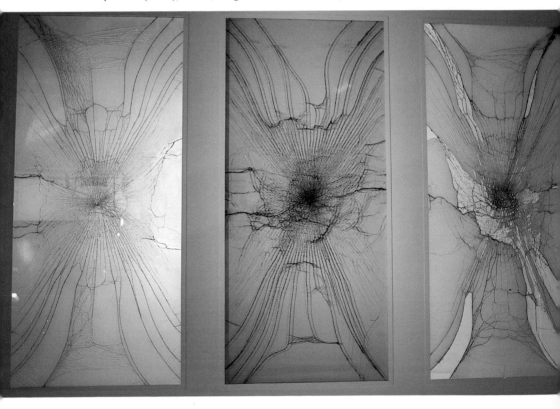

ALEXANDER BELESCHENKO

Alexander Beleschenko is probably the best-known British artist working in laminated glass today. Among his more notable commissions are ones for a stunning glass corridor in Canary Wharf, massive doors for the Herz Jesu Kirche in Munich and a 14 m high conical wall in Southwark tube station, London. This last project demonstrates one of the main problems facing artists working on the fault line between art and architecture. When Beleschenko was introduced to the Jubilee Line Extension's project managers as an artist back in the late 1990s, they were predictably nervous. The idea of lining a public space with a laminated glass artwork seemed to threaten all kinds of problems to do with public safety issues. When Beleschenko described himself as a 'cladding consultant' instead, everything was fine. His submission for Southwark was quickly accepted, and his pin-stripe-blue triangular panels now brighten the lives of the hundreds of thousands of people who walk under them on their way to the Tate Modern each year. Beleschenko takes a philosophical approach to the whole question of art-versus-cladding. 'What matters is that my work enriches the environment,' he says. 'Part of the brief that I give myself is to make something beautiful for the everyday world.'

RIGHT: *Southwark Station, detail*
BELOW: *Southwark Station*

Fusion Glass

If the industrial processes of a vast multi-national like Pilkington plc can provide a broad-brush inspiration for artists working with laminated glass, smaller commercial studios, such as Fusion Glass, offer a more direct source of ideas.

Unlike Pilkington, Fusion Glass makes its laminated products by a process known as cast-in-place (CIP) manufacture: a technique in which relatively small runs of glass are laminated by hand rather than by machine, with liquid resin being poured in between two layers of glass held apart by double-sided edging tape. Although it is unlikely that you will work on the same scale as a commercial studio like Fusion Glass, the methods that you will use to make your art will be exactly the same as theirs.

Fusion Glass produces mostly off-the-peg patterns, but can also provide bespoke glass for individual clients, most of which are architects. As well as applying a wide range of surface treatments to their glass – kiln texturing, sandblasting, gilding, acid etching and so on – the company also works with a number of laminating materials. Laminated products include Shattered Laminate, but Fusion has also sandwiched an impressive variety of other things between glass: muslins, silks and linens, paper, wood veneers and leaves. The studio's catalogue and website provide a good source of ideas for artists working with laminated glass.

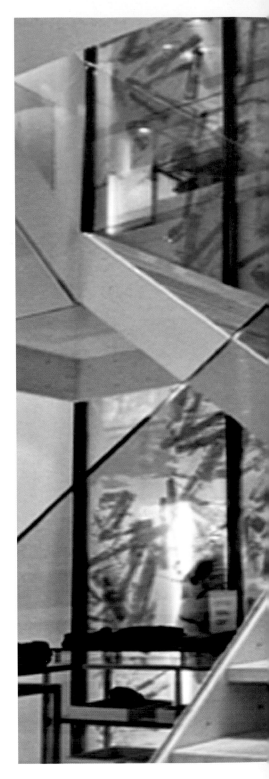

RIGHT: *Staircase, Daks shop, London; printed fabric by Michèle Oberdieck, laminated by Fusion Glass*

Glass, art and glass art: the case for anarchy

Derix Studios

If there is a heaven for glass artists, then it is probably in Taunusstein, an otherwise unheavenly village near Wiesbaden in Germany. Here, five generations of the Derix family have been helping glass artists make their art since the 1860s. Although there are other studios that specialise in working with artists, Derix is the place to which practitioners from all over the world turn when things get serious. Among other artists to have made the pilgrimage to Taunusstein are Patrick Heron, Graham Jones and Stephen Knapp.

It is particularly surprising, then, to find how small a role lamination has played in the output of Derix Studios generally. For the most part, artists working there have tended to use laminates as a way of making sure that large-scale pieces meet the various national safety standards (NSS) of the countries where the works will eventually end up.

Interior of Derix Studio Gallery, Germany

23

Patrick Heron, stained glass window, Tate St Ives

Thus Patrick Heron's piece in the foyer of Tate St Ives is laminated to make sure that it holds together safely rather than to exploit any aesthetic quality that laminates might have.

That said, Barbara Derix (deputy director of Derix Studios) is hugely excited about the potential that laminates have for artists working in glass. A few of the studios' more adventurous clients, like the Berlin-based artist Hella Santarossa, have already begun to experiment with glass lamination to make work that bears little or no resemblance to the traditional, well-behaved thing that we now think of as architectural glass.

During my recent visit to Derix Studios, an American glass artist gloomily confessed to me over lunch that he had 'had a breakage': the most dreadful thing that can happen to anyone working in unlaminated glass, and an accident that would delay his project – a vast rose window for a shopping centre in St Louis – by several days. It is this attitude to glass as a temperamental thing that has to be treated (often literally) with kid gloves that has led to glass artists having to work within set limits. I hope that anyone reading this book will see that lamination offers a way of getting around those limits and allowing glass to be used as the living, vibrant, sexy thing it is.

HELLA SANTAROSSA

One of the things you will find if you start working in laminated glass is that people do not know what to make of you. Since you work in panels and with colours, the easiest way to pigeonhole you will be as a stained-glass artist. That this is not a very satisfactory description is shown by the work of the Berlin based artist, Hella Santarossa. A member of the Derix family (of Derix Studios fame), Santarossa has had a successful international career as a painter, a sculptor and a film-maker. In the best family tradition, she also makes windows for churches. These are most definitely not stained glass, as shown by one recent window for a church in Heidelberg. Among other materials that Santarossa used in this project were photo-transfers of a swimmer's face, starfish, bits of shell and shards of light-reflecting glass. These were all incorporated in a thin layer of silicone resin which the artist had applied to her bottom sheet of glass in an open pour. In this way, the finished window manages to be not just painterly (as a traditional stained glass piece would be) but also sculptural: the objects contained in the space between the window's inner and outer panels give it a depth that fits in well with its underwater theme. At the same time, Santarossa's laminated window has another advantage over the traditional kind. Since silicone resins tend to stay relatively flexible over time, it will not be prone to the huge stresses of thermal expansion.

OPPOSITE: Church window in Heidelberg, by Hella Santarossa BELOW: Detail

CHAPTER FOUR

What is glass lamination?

In its broadest sense, as you will have seen, lamination means sticking together two or more thin sheets of just about anything: wood, stone or, in the case of this book, glass. This will be done using some kind of adhesive, usually a resin or glue. You will need to decide what kind of glass you are going to use and how you are going to stick your sheets together.

These decisions will be shaped by two main considerations: first, how you want your finished piece to look; and second, where it is going to go and how it is going to be used. If you are planning to make small-scale pieces for private use, then you can use more or less any materials you care to and laminate them in any way you like. If, on the other hand, you are thinking of making large-scale architectural works for use in public spaces, then you will have to take into account international safety requirements and questions of contractual durability.

Pre-laminated glass can be bought direct from a glass supplier and can be used on its own to make pieces. However, this book is primarily intended for the artist who wants to use the techniques of lamination as a process in itself, either in a private studio or in the glass department of an art school or college. We will now look at the primary materials in that process, namely glass and resin.

Choosing your glass

Given that glass has been around for 5000 years and has near-infinite practical applications, there are, as you might imagine, hundreds of different possible varieties for you to choose from, some of them ancient, some involving microchip technology. However, it is likely that you will want to begin by using relatively accessible and inexpensive glass, available from a local nonspecialist supplier.

Most glass that you buy in sheets from glass shops will be known as 'float' glass, having been manufactured by a process in which liquid glass is floated on molten tin. Within this category are two main subtypes, called soda-lime glass and lead glass respectively, according to their chemical composition.

Soda-lime glass

This glass, used in almost every kind of window, is by far the most commonly available. As you might expect, its main benefits are that it is easy to get hold of, can be found in all kinds of different thicknesses, is simple to have cut to size and cheap to buy. There are drawbacks, though.

The first is that – thanks to the presence of sodium oxide (Na_2O) in the chemical make-up of soda-lime glass – it expands and contracts easily with changes of

A stack of soda-lime glass

temperature. This means that it has to be dealt with carefully in studio conditions. Rapid changes of ambient temperature in your studio, especially if you are laminating two different kinds or thicknesses of glass to each other, can lead to your finished laminate being subjected to violent internal stresses. These, in turn, can lead to your laminate unsticking or 'delaminating', or even, in extreme cases, to cracking. Another drawback of soda-lime glass, and especially of its cheaper varieties, is that the presence of water-resistant calcium oxide (CaO) in its make-up tends to give it a greenish tinge.

Lead glass

As you would assume from the name, lead glass replaces the calcium oxide used in soda-lime glass with lead oxide (PbO). Under EEC rules, any glass with more than 25% lead oxide in it can call itself lead crystal; glass with 24% lead oxide or less tends to be known as crystal glass. The main advantage of lead glass is that, being sodium-free, it is much less prone to expansion and contraction, and is thus less likely to degrade. The second is that the removal of calcium oxide from its composition leaves it brilliantly clear and colourless. Lead glass is made in far smaller quantities than soda-lime glass, is harder to get hold of and is commensurately much more expensive.

Resins and glues

In the discussion on Pilkington plc, we saw that industrial manufacturers mostly laminate their glass by welding two or more layers together with pre-made sheets of polyvinyl butyral (PVB) in heated autoclaves. For studio purposes, laminating tends to be done by cast-in-place (CIP) methods, i.e. by hand and using liquid adhesives.

As with the kind of glass you choose, your choice of adhesive is going to have all kinds of implications both for your studio practice and for your finished piece. Glass is a dangerous material to work with for obvious reasons, but chemical resins and glues are also *extremely* hazardous, and have to be treated with respect. The chapter on health and safety should be read with care before you start laminating your first piece of glass.

Choosing your bonding process

Broadly speaking, glass can be laminated using one of two bonding processes, the first chemical, the second physical. Chemical bonding relies on the adhesive interaction of certain chemicals contained in resins and glues to stick your glass together. Physical bonding relies on the 'curing' of those resins or glues by exposure to ultraviolet light. Each of these processes has its advantages and disadvantages.

Chemical bonding

Liquid resins, based on polyester or silicone compounds, have been around for about 20 years now. Generally speaking, they consist of a base resin which remains liquid under normal conditions, but which can be made to harden over a period of time and to a set consistency by the addition of one or more additives, bonding your glass together. Liquid

An open pour in progress, Derix Studios

resins of this kind can be used in one of two ways, both of them relatively simple.

Open-pour laminating
In this, a plane of glass is laid flat and a raised edge or dam of double-sided adhesive tape built up all the way around the area or areas of glass you want to laminate. Your pre-mixed resin is then poured into the dammed area(s) and a second pane placed on top of the first, forming an airtight seal. The big advantage of open-pour laminating is that it

allows different areas of glass on a single panel to be laminated using (for example) different coloured resins. The main disadvantage is that it is tricky to do without either overfilling or under-filling the dammed areas: the first will result in overspill when the top panel of glass is applied, the second in a non-air-tight seal which will lead to all kinds of subsequent structural problems with your piece. Works made using the open-pour process are also prone to contamination with dust and other foreign bodies.

Envelope laminating
In this, your sheets of glass are formed into a pocket (or 'envelope') by applying the same double-sided adhesive tape as before around the edges of the panel, with a small space left untaped along one edge for the insertion of the resin, and gaps at either end of this edge to allow air to escape once the resultant envelope begins to fill up. The taped glass is then tilted at an angle and the already-prepared resin poured in or injected through the open space until the gap between the two sheets is filled. The envelope is then given an airtight seal using a silicone sealant. If you laminate one sheet of glass to another in a single pour, you will end up with a one-face laminate. If you laminate one sheet of glass between two others, you will get a two-face laminate. Each pour has to be done in two pouring stages, separated by at least 24 hours.

As with the open-pour method, problems can arise if either too little or too much resin is used. The principal disadvantage of envelope laminating is that whole panels of glass have to be treated in one go, so this limits the possibility of treating of different areas of the glass with different resins.

Warning It should be noted here that the use of liquid resins in making pieces is still largely experimental. Although good guides exist for the use of resin laminates in commercial applications, art-glass lamination still involves a great deal of trial and error. Different practitioners favour different resins: I have tended to use polyester resins, for example, while Derix Studios are suffi-ciently confident about the silicone-based resins they use to offer 30-year guarantees on the structural integrity of their laminated pieces. If all this sounds a little scary, then reflect that working in laminated glass does at least allow for real novelty and real discovery.

Injection laminating
As its name implies, this method of lami-nating involves introducing your resin into your laminate through a disposable hypodermic syringe or via a hand-pump. You may want to use one or other of these methods if you are making smaller-scale pieces: try to prise apart the top edge of, say, a 200 mm x 200 mm taped glass panel with an open funnel and boning sticks and you will either unstick your envelope or crack your glass.

To make an injection laminate, tape your glass as before but this time leave only two small gaps, one at either end of the top edge. One of these gaps will be used for inserting the thin plastic tube attached to the end of your resin-filled syringe; the other will act as an air vent so that air can be expelled as the enve-lope fills with resin. (It is a good idea to

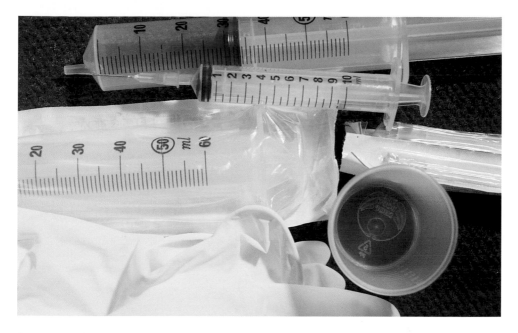

keep a supply of hypodermic syringes in the studio. They are useful for all kinds of things, including measuring additives, filling in air bubbles and part-colouring resins. Syringes can be bought from any chemist, as can the thin plastic tubes which are normally used for rinsing out waxy ears.) Insert your tube, inject the resin slowly and evenly until the envelope is full, remove the tube and plug the remaining gaps with silicone as before.

For intermediate-sized pieces (around 350 mm x 350 mm) a syringe may be too small and slow a means of injecting your resin. In this case, you can use one of those small hand-pumps sold by garden centres for spraying shrubs with pesticides instead. The only trouble with this is that pumps are fiddly to clean, and need to be cleaned thoroughly every time you use them or they will clog up. While syringes are cheap enough to throw away after one use, pumps are not.

Keep a good supply of syringes in your studio

Ultraviolet bonding

Sheets of glass can also be bonded together by curing (or hardening) resins with ultraviolet-A (UVA) light. This is not as exotic as it sounds: a wide variety of suitable UV glues and resins, such as Uvekol, exists on the market, as does a selection of affordable UV lamps. What is more, ultraviolet bonding is reputed to have certain advantages over chemical bonding: the resins used are said to be more stable and less toxic than conventional resins, are clearer when cured, are available commercially in a variety of colours and do not yellow with age. UV bonding can also be done in about 20 minutes.

CHRISSY HARFLEET

For the Sussex-based artist Chrissy Harfleet, resins are only part of the story. In any given artwork, Harfleet will trap chains, wires, powdered pigments and pieces of coloured glass between two or more sheets of float glass and then fire the whole lot in a kiln at 800°C. When this is done, she will laminate the resultant artwork between two more sheets of unslumped glass, experimenting with all kinds of different resins – polyesters, clear casting resins, silicone and UV bonding resins – in which she has included yet more pigments and objects. The results are incredibly rich and complex, layered like an archaeological dig. It was precisely this ability to (as the artist puts it) 'freeze time in space' that led Harfleet into lamination in the first place.

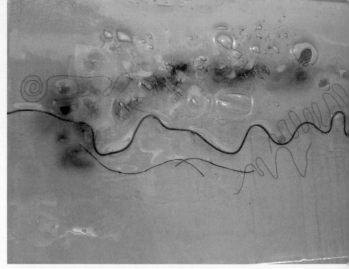

ABOVE: 'Dangerwater', Chrissy Harfleet

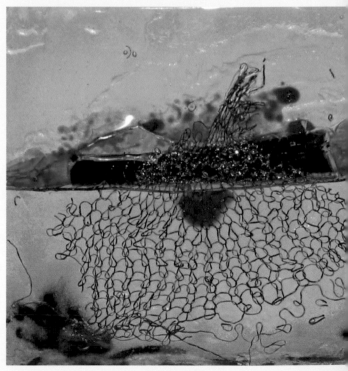

'Wave', Chrissy Harfleet OPPOSITE: 'Crackle Leaf', Chrissy Harfleet

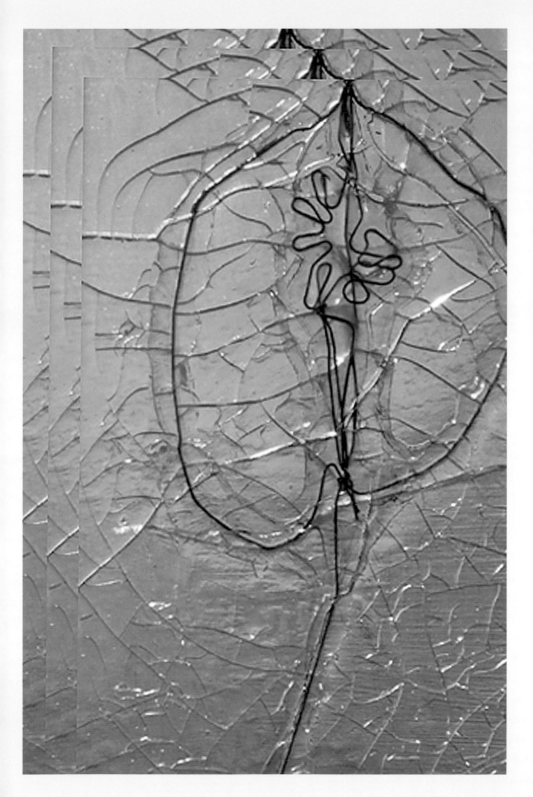

CHAPTER FIVE

Step-by-step

In this chapter, we are going to learn how to laminate a basic sheet of glass to another basic sheet of glass using liquid resin. Whatever the scale you decide to work on in the future and however sophisticated the materials you choose to use, the procedures you learn now will be the ones that carry you through the rest of your laminating career: so make sure you are clear about all the issues at this point.

I have found that it is a good idea to go back to basics whenever starting any new type of work, so the good laminating studio should have lots of test pieces propped up against its walls. It is always better to find out about any new problems you may be about to face on your own test panel rather than on one that a client is paying you £10,000 for.

What you will need before your start

If the following list looks a little on the intimidating side, note that most suppliers of glass resins will provide potential glass laminators with a cheap starter kit to go with their first drum of resin. The resins themselves are not particularly cheap: a 20 kg drum currently costs around £300, and is not available in smaller sizes. All the equipment included in the list below will be explained as we go along, as will its use.

1 x 20.5 kg drum of resin
2 x 120 ml bottles organic peroxide resin additive
2 x bottles organosilane ester adhesion promoter (optional)
3 x 66 m rolls 0.8 mm clear double-sided adhesive tape
2 x 33 m rolls 1.6 mm clear double-sided adhesive tape
2 x measuring jugs
2 x plastic pouring jugs
1 x 50 ml open funnel
1 x 125 ml closed funnel
1 x 5 kg container resin cleaner
4 x boning sticks
10 x hypodermic needles
2 x hypodermic syringes

Since you will be working with a variety of highly dangerous materials as a glass laminator, it also makes sense to equip yourself with protective clothing, gloves, goggles and first-aid equipment right from the outset.

Laminating a test panel

Before you start playing around with more sophisticated laminating techniques, it will be as well to laminate a simple, square plain-glass-to-plain-glass panel so as to familiarise yourself with the processes involved. For purposes of ease, I would recommend that you either cut

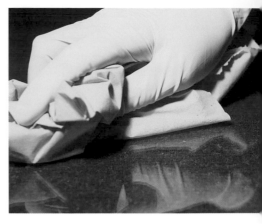

Cleaning your glass with methylated spirits, wearing surgical gloves

Materials for cleaning your glass

two 500 mm x 500 mm sheets of cheap, 3 mm or 4 mm thick float glass yourself, or that you have them cut for you.

Cleaning and laying the glass

Before going any further, there is one word that you need to have in your mind at all times when working with laminates and that word is: CLEAN. No matter how strong your resins, they will only adhere to glass that is absolutely clean. Use them with dirty glass and you will find that your panels either do not stick at all, or that they rapidly begin to unstick. Never touch glass with your fingers; always wear surgical gloves.

Given that cast-in-place laminating needs to be done as precisely as possible, it is also good to have a strong wooden board on which to rest your panel during and after resin pouring. This board should be covered with thick fabric (old carpet is ideal) to prevent scratching of the glass. You should also make sure that the board, and the table on which it will eventually be left to lie, are absolutely flat: do this by checking both with spirit-levels along their length and breadth. If your newly-laminated panel is left to lie on an uneven surface, you add to the risk of the uncured resin migrating away from raised areas, a sure-fire way of ending up with problems.

Put on your surgical gloves and lay the first of your sheets of glass on the board. Now take the first of three clean cloths and wet it thoroughly with methylated spirits. (Specialist glass-cleaning paper is available from glass suppliers, although I find old cotton sheets are easier to use.) Wipe the upper face of the glass until no smears are left, then leave any excess meths to evaporate. Repeat the process using a second, less wet cloth. Finally, buff your glass with a dry cloth, making sure that absolutely no dirt or foreign objects (dust, grease, threads, hairs) are left on the surface. Prepare your second sheet of glass in the same way. If you are going to use an adhesion promoter – a chemical that, as its name suggests, helps things to stick to each other – then do so now.

Taping the glass

Now we are going to apply the double-sided adhesive tape around the perimeter of the glass. This tape comes in various thicknesses, though I find that 1.6 mm is the easiest to work with. Glass tapes of this kind only stick effectively if they are applied at a temperature of 20°C or higher, so check that your studio is warm enough before you begin. Tapes must also be kept dry, so make sure that they are stored in airtight conditions.

Glass tapes come on a roll, one side of which is masked with release paper. Unroll strips of tape, glue-side down, all the way along the left and right edges of the glass, flush with them, pressing down firmly to make sure the tape has stuck; then cut it to the exact size with a scalpel. Now do the same thing along the top and bottom edges of the glass, but this time leaving a gap of 2 mm at either end. Pull back and crease the eight cut ends of the release paper to a distance of 40 mm or so each. This will allow you to position your upper sheet of glass precisely, corner-to-corner, on top of the lower sheet. Do this, pressing down to make sure that the tape has stuck on both sides. Once this is done, pull the remaining release paper away from the tape on the right, left and bottom edges of your panel, leaving the paper on the tape running along the top edge for the time being. Press along the

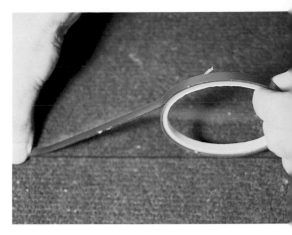

Applying the double-sided tape to your bottom sheet

Cutting the tape with a scalpel

Pressing the tape down with end of scalpel

39

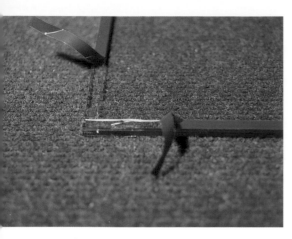

Peeling off release paper from the corners

Positioning the top sheet of glass

Removing remaining release tape using a suction pad

taped edges once again to make sure that they are firmly stuck. Glass tapes take a minimum of 30 minutes to adhere properly, so leave your panel to sit for this time.

Applying the silicone

Once the tape has set, take a silicone gun containing clear silicone sealant and fill in the two gaps at either corner of the bottom edge of your panel. (Ordinary silicone sealant from a do-it-yourself shop is fine for this procedure.) If you are making a larger panel, or if you want to be absolutely sure that no leakage will occur, then you can continue the silicone seal all the way around the left, right and bottom edges of your panel, smearing the silicone with your thumb to ensure that the seal is complete. Leave the top edge and its two gaps unsealed for the moment. Silicone takes four to five hours to dry, and this is the minimum time for which your panel should now be left. You will now have an envelope of glass, sealed on three sides and left open on the fourth.

Preparing your resin

Before touching any commercial resin, you must always read the manufacturer's instructions that come with it. Most resins are dangerous when inhaled and peroxide-based additives can burn you badly. It cannot be stressed enough that good studio practice needs to be followed at all times while you are laminating glass.

A variety of different resins are available on the commercial market. Most of these resins are two-part compounds, which rely on the introduction of additives to make them set or 'cure' (i.e. to turn them from pourable liquids into bonded solids). The proportion of additive to resin will vary from product to product, but also according to the properties you want your cured resin to have: for example, whether you want your final product to be more or less rigid or flexible. Your supplier should also provide you with a manual outlining the different variants possible with your particular product. The proportion of additive to resin will vary according to how quickly or slowly you need your resin to set, and according to the ambient temperature of your studio.

The other thing you will have to calculate is the amount of resin you will need for your particular piece. Obviously, this will vary according to the size of the work involved. When calculating the amount of resin required, you will need to take into account three variables: the length and breadth of the panel and the thickness of the adhesive tape used. In the case of your 500 mm x 500 mm x 1.6 mm test piece, for example, this will work out at 380 ml. Manufacturers also tend to suggest that you add an extra 25 ml to your recipe to compensate for resin left behind in your pouring jug; your final amount for this particular panel will thus be 405 ml.

Note that manufacturers' instructions generally assume you will be laminating flat glass to flat glass. If you are including uneven or absorbent materials like wood or cloth in your work, or if you are laminating textured glass (like the shattered panels I often use), then you will have to include more resin than the manuals suggest to cope with increased internal surface area. I tend to include

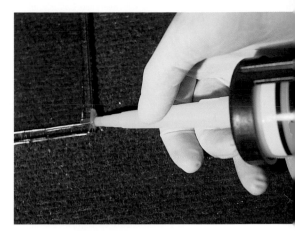

Applying silicone sealant from a gun

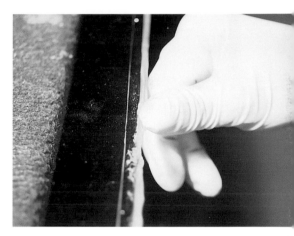

Smearing the sealant into the edge of the glass with your thumb

20–25% more resin than the manufacturers recommend.

Once you have calculated the amounts of base resin and additives that you will need, pour the required resin into a clean plastic measuring jug. It is good practice to do this through a fine sieve, preferably of muslin: this is especially important if your resin is old or the tin has been opened for some time. Whisk the resin briskly for a minute or so with a stick or spatula, removing any air bubbles that rise to the surface with

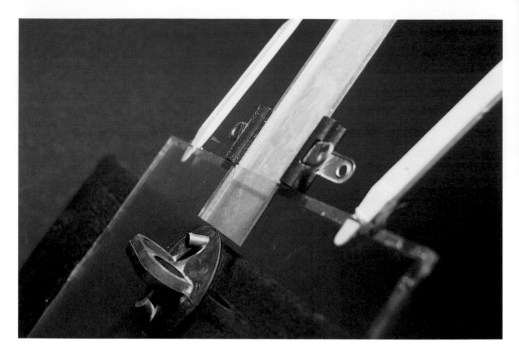

Inserting boning sticks and open funnel

BELOW: Tilting the board on brick props

absorbent paper. Now stir in the required amount of additive. Always cover the jug of finished resin to stop foreign objects from falling into it.

Tilting the board

The prepared resin is going to be poured into the unsealed top edge of your glass envelope through a flat metal channel known as an open funnel. To ensure that the liquid resin feeds itself evenly across the envelope, you will have to tilt it at an angle of 45°: gravity will do the rest. First, you need to insert a pair of flat plastic dividers, known as 'boning sticks', into the envelope's open top edge and over the still-masked adhesive tape. These will hold the two sheets of glass apart sufficiently for you to insert the open funnel between the two boning sticks.

Once you have done this, carefully hammer two nails into the board on which your glass is resting along the bottom edge of the panel; wrap these nails in foam rubber with a piece of masking tape. When you tilt the board up to 45°, the panel will rest on these padded nails. The board can be held up at 45° using bricks or blocks of wood, with a pair of sandbags supporting it along its bottom edge. (If you are going to be making large-scale panels on a regular basis, you might think about investing in a tilting table.) Make sure you have your silicone gun to hand.

Pouring the resin

Now begin to pour your pre-prepared liquid resin, slowly and carefully, into the open funnel. The resin will fill the cavity between the two sheets of glass more or less evenly until it comes roughly halfway up the envelope.

When all the resin is done, remove the boning sticks and open funnel and carefully wipe the inside edges of your glass with absorbent paper. Make sure that no resin is left on the glass, or the final strip of adhesive tape will not stick to it.

Once you have made sure that the glass is absolutely clean, remove the remaining release paper from the last strip of tape and squeeze the two edges of the glass together firmly until you are sure that they are stuck to each other. Then, removing one set of bricks or blocks at a time, gently lower the board until it is flat. The resin will seep slowly towards the top edge of the glass, expelling trapped air through the two remaining 2 mm gaps. As soon as the resin reaches the second of these – it will

Liquid resin being poured into an envelope through an open funnel

tend to hit one gap before the other – plug them both with a squirt of silicone. Then continue your silicone seal along the final edge of your panel, smearing it with your thumb as before. You will now have an airtight glass sandwich, which should be left to lie, untouched and perfectly flat, for at least 24 hours before it is moved.

This is your first laminated glass piece: congratulations.

43

Things you can do with laminates

Although you have now made your first laminated glass piece, the panel in question may strike you as a little dull. Luckily, there are all kinds of other materials and techniques you can use to liven things up.

In fact, just about anything can be used in the glass laminating process.

This chapter will look at a few of the more creative ways in which you can push the boundaries of art-glass lamination: one of the most exciting things about the medium is that you can (and will) find many more as you go along. As you do so, though, always bear in mind that resins are not really made with artists in mind, and that you should always test new materials and/or procedures in the studio before unleashing them on an unsuspecting client. Also remember that resins and their additives are potentially dangerous chemicals, and that some of the things you may think of adding to them may turn out to be bad for them (and you).

Things to do with resins

Adding colour

The first thing you will probably want to do with your plain glass 'canvas' is to introduce an element of colour. One way

to do this, obviously, is by using coloured glass. The problem with this is that commercial coloured glass is made with decorative (rather than artistic) ends in mind, by applying a thin coat of tinted pigment to plain glass. As a result, the colours tend to be a bit on the thin side. Another problem with working in coloured glass is that you have to use your colour in hard-edged patches, since you will effectively be making a glass mosaic or, if you prefer, stained glass. Without any disrespect to stained-glass artists, it was exactly this kind of inflexibility that made me want to experiment with laminates in the first place.

A more adaptable way of introducing colour into your work will be by tinting your resin. Most manufacturers of resins also make a range of colourants to go with them and, helpfully, these come in a variety of finishes: transparent, translucent, opaque, metallic and pearl, to name the most common. You can mix and match these in any way you choose, just as you would any other pigment.

Of course, you will still need to use your common sense in making sure that different pigments made by the same manufacturer, or pigments made by different manufacturers, are compatible with each other. If you use too much transparent colourant, then your resin will not set. If you use too little metallic colourant, the resultant colour will not be UV-stable, i.e. it will quickly fade when exposed to light. If in doubt, always consult your suppliers.

Streaking or marbling your resin interlayer

This process is carried out in two stages – one open pour and one envelope pour – and over a two-day period. The glass has to be left horizontal for at least 48 hours, so make sure that space is kept free for it. During the first 24-hour period, your resin-covered glass is left open to the elements: it is a good idea to leave it somewhere where there is not going to be dust floating about.

On the first day, clean and tape your glass as for a regular pour, but omitting the gaps in the adhesive tape dam running around the perimeter. Measure out enough resin to produce a thin surface covering on your bottom glass (about 1200 ml per square metre). Into this resin, pour your pre-prepared colourant at whatever dilution you wish to use. Either stir this a couple of times with a clean glass rod or pour the unstirred resin/colourant mixture back and forth between two jugs until you get a streaked effect you like the look of; then pour your mixture onto the prepared glass, playing around with patterns as you go. Pouring the resin in straight lines, about 100 mm apart and parallel to the longest edge, produces the best results. These strips will slowly merge into each other, and colours will continue to settle and disperse according to the thickness of your mixture until the resin is set. You can also use syringes to squirt streaks or blobs or anything else you like into the resin at this point. You can think of the whole process as a kind of horizontal abstract painting. Once you have finished, leave the panel to dry.

The next day, prepare a clear resin/additive mixture, place your second sheet of glass on top of the first, tilt the panel and proceed as for a normal envelope pour. Do not panic if your upper sheet of glass touches the still-tacky streaked resin as you put it on: although this will cause temporary air bubbles to appear, these will quickly disappear as the fresh, clear resin fills the envelope and pushes the two sheets apart.

For a marbled effect on your interlayer, follow the same procedure as above but use two different coloured resins (rather than one clear and one coloured) in your initial pour. Note that a mixture of black and amber pigments can produce a nice-looking tortoise-shell effect.

Adding other things to your resin

You can add just about anything you like to resins, as long as the thing in question is fine and dry, for example: glitter, small chips of gold foil, coffee, tea leaves, seeds and sand, to name but a few. Obviously, you will need to experiment in the studio with small test panels to see how your additives look and whether they work in practice. Moist things, for example wet rather than dry tea leaves, tend not to work because they react badly with the resin and stop it setting. Equally, if you add too much of any material, or pieces that are too large, then you run the risk of spoiling your laminate and the whole thing falling apart sooner or later.

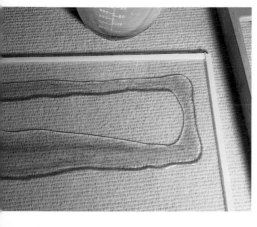

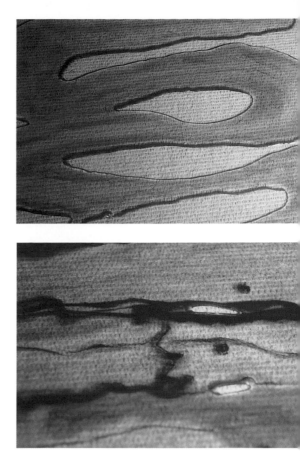

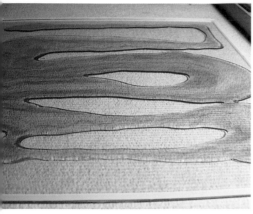

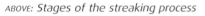
ABOVE: Stages of the streaking process

Dry tea leaves mixed in with the resin

Materials that can be included in your laminate

As well as stirring colouring agents, coffee or semolina into your resins, you can also use lamination to sandwich larger things between the layers of glass in your envelope.

Leaves and grasses

Leaves and grasses are two of the more familiar materials for inclusion in laminates. As with all organic materials, the most important thing is to make sure that your leaves or grasses are absolutely dry. This can be done using a wooden

47

botanical press and blotting paper, and then leaving your pressed materials in a warm, dry place until you are sure that they are absolutely moisture-free. If they are not, then they may prevent your resin from curing or react badly with it later on, causing all kinds of problems.

You can work with leaves in one of two ways. First, you can simply glue them to a sheet of glass using dabs of silicone and use this as the bottom sheet in a normal envelope pour. Obviously, the pouring needs to be done gently so that your leaf does not come adrift or break up. This is one of the drawbacks of this procedure, the other being that your dots of silicone glue will be faintly visible in the finished panel.

One way around this is to try a second method, which is to do a shallow open pour (as you might if you were streaking your resin). Here, leaves are pressed into a thin initial layer of wet resin which is then left to dry; this then becomes the bottom sheet of your finished panel. An advantage of this is that there are no visible glue dots, and you can build up several layers of leaves or other materials in a collage effect. The main disadvantage of using this method is that panels made with an open pour are less stable than ones made by an envelope pour, and that the pouring process is generally messier.

TOP LEFT: Dried leaves laminated by the injection method

LEFT: Dried leaves laminated using the shallow open pour method

OPPOSITE: Dried grasses laminated by the injection method

Laminated Japanese rice paper

Paper and wood veneers

The image above shows a test piece made using Japanese rice paper. Although you would think that resin, being liquid, would make paper disintegrate, it does just the opposite: it stabilises the paper and makes it semi-translucent, bringing out all the richness and subtlety of the laid weave.

As with leaves and grasses, you can simply glue your bits of paper in a collaged layer to the bottom sheet of glass using a silicone adhesive and then do a normal envelope pour. If you are using a single sheet of paper the same size and shape as your glass, you can prepare your bottom panel by using 0.8 mm (rather than 1.6 mm) double-sided adhesive tape instead, peeling the release-backing off the tape and then sticking your paper to this all the way around the edges. You then apply another layer of 0.8 mm tape to the upper surface of your paper, remove the release-backing, press your upper panel of glass onto this and seal the edges of the resultant envelope with silicone sealant. The panel is then filled with resin using a hypodermic syringe or hand-pump. This technique can also be applied to fine wood veneers.

Fabrics

The following images show works which include fabrics in the laminating process. The first is of a test panel made using a piece of material by the textile designer Margo Selby of 'Looming Marvellous'. The second was made by Michèle Oberdieck, who has her own textiles laminated into glass panels. These have recently been incorporated into a staircase at the DAKS shop in New Bond

50

Laminated wood veneers and sheet metal

BELOW: Laminated fabric designed by 'Looming Marvellous'

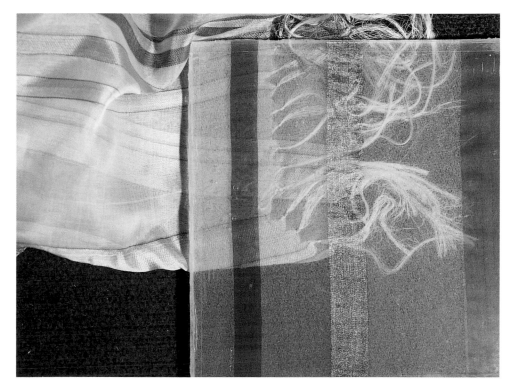

'Leaf' laminated fabric, designed by Michèle Oberdieck

BELOW: 'Floral' laminated fabric, designed by Michèle Oberdieck

Street, London, although they could also be used as shower doors, table tops or simply as artworks to hang on the wall. Oberdieck prints her laminated fabrics with devoré, rubber flocking, pigments and washes, which gives them layer upon layer of depth and movement.

Air

Although air bubbles can appear in your resin interlayer by accident, they can also be put there by design.

To work with air bubbles, prepare your glass panel as for a normal envelope pour. Instead of completely filling the interlayer with resin, however, you pour in only (for example) two-thirds of the normal required amount. Once this is done, plug your air vents with silicone as usual and lower your panel until it is flat. You will now have a single large air-pocket trapped in your envelope, and this pocket can be broken down into smaller bubbles simply by moving the panel around gently. When you have an effect you like the look of, stop: the resin will set with the air bubbles trapped permanently inside it.

Clear bubbles are beautiful in themselves, but they can also be filled with coloured resins to create a variety of different effects. To do this, you will have to wait until your initial resin layer is semi-set; once it is, the bubbles trapped inside it can be injected with other coloured resins using a hypodermic syringe. You will need to do a lot of experimenting with this technique. If you inject your secondary resin too early, i.e. before your initial resin layer has begun to set, then the two resins will simply run into each other and produce a blobby mess. If you

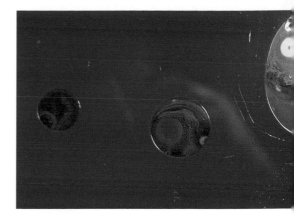

Red coloured piece with air bubbles trapped in resin

Green coloured resin with trapped air bubbles

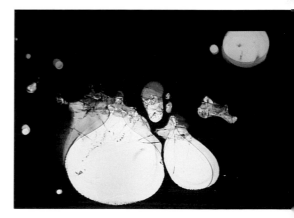

Coloured resin with trapped air bubbles laminated onto a broken sheet

53

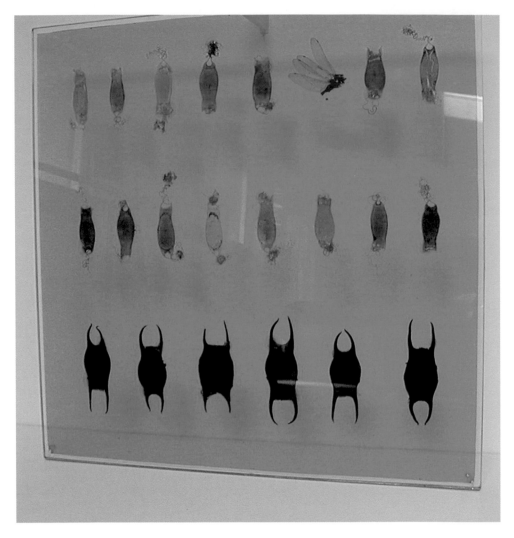

Igloo's mermaids' purses laminated with coloured resin

wait too long to inject your secondary resin, your initial interlayer will have hardened and your hypodermic needle will either not get through it or will leave an unsightly needle-track if it does.

Other things

The list of materials you can include in your laminates is pretty well endless: so here is just a single example of an unexpected material that caught my eye at a recent trade fair.

Paul Thompson runs a specialist glass company called Igloo from a farmhouse in North Wales. Among many other things that Igloo has included in its laminates are so-called mermaid's purses, which Thompson finds on beaches and then dries in leaf-presses. In Igloo's 'Mermaid's Purse' product, the objects hang in the resin as though they are floating in the sea: a delightful

Laminated grasses with coloured resin by Igloo

effect, that plays on the inherent ambiguities of resin in glass.

Things to do with your glass

So far, we have looked at resin as the major ingredient in the glass-resin recipe. Of course, the other ingredient is glass itself. As you will have gathered, there are dozens of different types of glass that you can use for lamination: float, toughened, patterned, antique and so on. But there are also things you can do to your glass that lend themselves particularly well to the laminating process.

Breaking your sheets

Whatever its eventual use, the whole point of lamination is to stick things together. Among other things that can be stuck together in this way are bits of broken glass.

Design transferred to glass sheets

Smashing in progress

OPPOSITE: *'Orange Gerberas', Yorgos Studio (2002)*

Pre-laminated glass can be broken in a variety of different ways: with a hammer, with a gun, with a blowtorch and with all kinds of other things. The patterns that breakage produces can be extraordinarily beautiful: delicate or violent, strong or subtle, with widely differing paths of light. They can be used as the canvas for all kinds of other interventions with paints, spray-paints, pastels, inks and anything else you might think of.

Best of all, there is the fact that breaking laminated glass involves a creative mix of control and accident. First, work out a concept sketch on paper, then block this up and transfer it to your sheet of laminated glass using specialist glass crayons. Once this is done, choose a point somewhere along one of the lines

in the crayoned sketch to make your first hammer-blow (using a regular household hammer). This initial blow will produce a familiar star-shaped shatter-pattern, with cracks radiating out of it in various directions. Look for the crack that most nearly follows the crayoned line you have drawn, and then encourage the crack to follow that line by hitting along it, gently, with a finer hammer. Once the first line is finished, you can start on a second, and so on until the whole sketch is completed.

As you can imagine, part of the joy of this process lies in the unexpected. Your major lines may suddenly join themselves together with a network of little cracks

OPPOSITE: 'Red Hot Pokers', Yorgos Studio (2002)

RIGHT TOP: 'Aerial View', Yorgos Studio (2001)

RIGHT BELOW: 'Yellow Lilies', Yorgos Studio (2001)

you had not intended to be there, or a tiny chip of glass may fall out of the panel altogether at the point where two lines intersect. Generally speaking, these little accidents give the work a spontaneity it might have lacked if it had been made under perfectly controlled conditions. You can apply pigments to the finished crack-pattern, rubbing them in or pouring them on according to their nature and wiping away any excess once the cracks have finished absorbing the pigments. When the panel is dry, either use it as the bottom sheet of a one-face laminate (i.e. an envelope with a single sheet of unbroken glass on top), or as an interlayer between two sheets of unbroken glass (a two-face laminate, which requires a double pour).

Another way of using broken glass is to smash it after the event. The Welsh glass studio Igloo makes a product called 'Smashed Ice' in which a layer of toughened glass is laminated between two layers of regular float glass. Once the panel is cured, a metal pick is placed against the exposed edge of the toughened glass and tapped sharply with a hammer. Due to the nature of the laminate, the interlayer panel will shatter completely without weakening the structure of the panel.

Cutting your panels

So far, we have taken for granted the fact that your sheet of glass will stay as it is, i.e. that if you begin with a 500 mm x 500 mm square panel, then you will

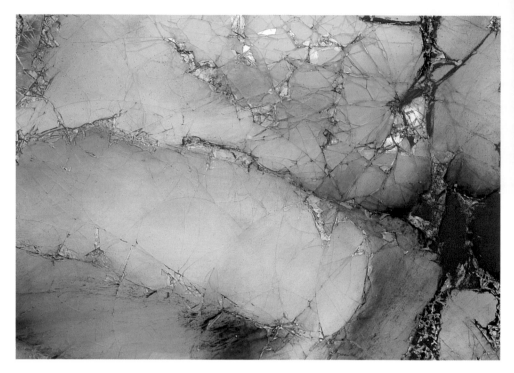

'Open Water Dive 1', Yorgos Studio (2003)   BELOW: *'Thames', Yorgos Studio (2003)*

Shattered bar-top by Igloo Glass

end up with a 500 mm x 500 mm square panel. However, the whole point of glass lamination is to produce a sandwich of glass which is just as strong as it would be if it were a single pane; and, just as single panes of glass can be cut to different sizes and shapes, so can laminated ones. If you want an amoeba-shaped artwork, then you can cut your finished panel using regular glass-cutting tools, or you can have it cut for you.

Of course, there are problems. A laminate that incorporates mermaid's purses or tea leaves or air bubbles or panels of shattered glass is never going to be as strong as the straightforward, flat-on-flat product of a resin manufacturer's dreams. If you cut your finished laminate or drill holes into it, then you are going to weaken the panel and increase the chances of it breaking.

JAMES CARPENTER

The whole point of laminated glass is that it should not break, and many artists have found inspiration in this fact. One of these is the New York-based American artist James Carpenter. Carpenter, one of the most successful people currently working in the medium, exploits the sense of security that laminated glass is meant to embody. Most tempered glass is made for use in the new curtain wall structures that have dominated large-scale civic building of the last 40 years or so. Carpenter's work plays with this fact to blur the line between architecture and art, and by doing so to redefine that strange phrase 'architectural glass'. One of his most spectacular pieces, a work in Hong Kong called 'Suspended Glass Tower' (1998), consists of a building-within-a-building, a piece of art that is bolted together using all the precision of a laminated glass skyscraper, and which sits in the entrance lobby of such a skyscraper. The piece's power lies in its exactness – in Carpenter's meticulous and elegant appliance of science.

But it also comes from the fact that we do not know quite what to make of the piece, how to define it. In the most beautiful way imaginable, it takes certainty and makes it uncertain.

'Suspended Glass Tower',
James Carpenter (1998):
RIGHT: Detail

CHAPTER SEVEN

Testing and record-keeping

As we have seen, art-glass lamination is still at an experimental stage. As a result, it is prone to surprises (some of them nasty) that better-known media, like oil paints, are not. The upshot of this is that you should always test any kind of new procedure or material before you use it in commissioned work, or in any piece you are making for sale. And since longevity is always going to be an issue in pieces made in a medium whose shelf life is largely unknown, it is also a good idea to be scrupulous about your record-keeping.

Having a logbook for each work that comes out of your studio is not going to stop that work from fading or delaminating or whatever other disaster might befall it: but a logbook may at least help you figure out what went wrong and why.

Testing your pieces

Obviously, you cannot make a preliminary test piece for every single work you do. In any case, chances are that you will end up making the same kind of work again and again over an extended period, so that you will be familiar enough with its particular problems without testing them first. Whenever you know that you are going to be working in a different way or introducing new materials, you should make a simple, small-scale test piece as a matter

of course. The longer in advance you make this piece, the longer you will have to see if anything goes wrong with it in the studio. Where at all possible, keep test samples for three months, examining them every couple of weeks to make sure that they are not degrading.

Needless to say, things can begin to go wrong with pieces long after three months have passed, and problems will be different in larger pieces where the stresses and pressures are different from those in small sample panels. Equipment at Pilkington plc subjects samples of the company's laminated glass to decades' worth of wear and tear in the course of a day or so, to look at the effect on the glass of long-term exposure to the elements. On a less sophisticated level, Derix Studios has dozens of test panels propped up against its outside walls to check for signs of fading or thermal cracking or resin failure.

Keeping your notes

It is a good idea to work out a standard note-keeping form which can be kept on a computer and printed off as and when needed. Every piece of work – test piece or finished panel, large or small, complex or simple – has its record, a kind of logbook in miniature. An example record-keeping form is shown on page 65.

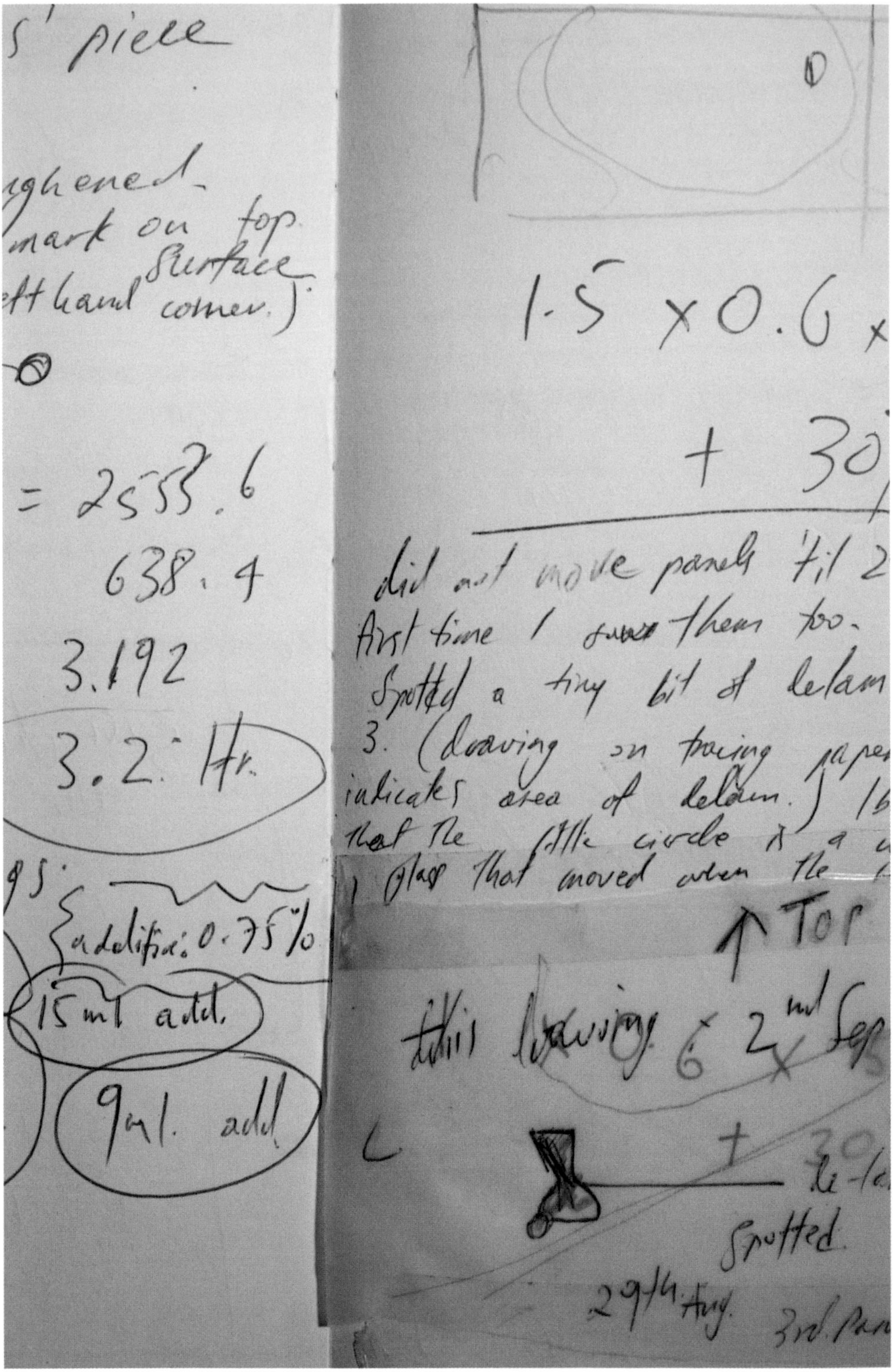

s' piece

ughened.
mark on top.
ft hand surface
corner.)

= 2553.6
638.4
3.192
3.2 Hr.

95
addition: 0.75%
15 ml add.
9ml. add

1.5 × 0.6 ×

+ 30

did not move panels 'til 2
first time I saw them too.
Spotted a tiny bit of delam
3. (drawing on tracing paper
indicates area of delam.) 16
that the little circle × a u
glass that moved when the 1

↑ Top
this drawing 6 2nd Sep
+ 30
Re-la
Spotted.
29th Aug. 3rd Pan

Name / title of piece: "Flames'	GLASS used: 6.4 lam + 6mm.
Dimensions: 2.4 m x 0.7 m.	middle sheet / canvas: 6.4 lam
Start Date: Jan. '03	front face: 6mm Float.
Finishing Date (final pour): Aug. 03.	back face: ———,

Diagram of face 1

clear. / clear / clear

Description / process used on face 1:   Date: 18th Feb. 03

S/blasted. / break / Sandseal /
pigments –

Materials used (in order of application):   Date: 05 Apr. 03 –
List of pigments: foil blue.   25th July 03
Sandseal. Black

Resin Calculations (face 1):   Pigments in resin:
2.4 x 0.7 x 1520 = 2553.6.
+30 % extra (766.08) + 3319.68 = 3.4 litre.

Resin amount for face 1:	3.4 litre
Additive amount for face 1:	1% ⇒ 34 ml.
Date of laminating face 1:	28th July 03
Tape used: 16mm.	Studio Temperature: 18°C.

Observations during lamination: fine

Observations after lamination: dates, de-lamination, causes, diagram,

fine

Record-keeping form

CHAPTER EIGHT

Health and safety

One of the great pleasures of working with laminated glass is that you will be making artworks out of industrial materials and using industrial processes. However, this same fact also means that laminating can be an extremely hazardous thing to do.

Many of the chemicals used in glass resins and resin additives are either potentially damaging to health or dangerous to handle or both. Because these resins and additives are really intended for use in factories or professional glass studios, they take certain things for granted: that you will be trained in the handling of the chemicals they contain, and be aware of their dangers; that you will wear respirators, goggles and other protective clothing when using them; that there will be proper ventilation and extraction systems in your workplace; that you will have access to trained first-aid personnel in case of an accident, and/or know how to deal with the chemicals yourself should anything go wrong; and that you will be working in an environment that is regularly checked by a health and safety professional to make sure all of the above precautions are observed.

Obviously, most of these things will not apply to the single artist working in the studio. However, most of these health and safety practices can (and

must) be replicated on a small scale, and this chapter looks at ways of doing so.

The dangers of resins

Toxic chemicals

Most resins and resin additives are *highly* toxic, and you must familiarise yourself with manufacturers' instructions and safety procedures before handling them. Their use can be dangerous in both the short- and long-term. Here is a brief guide to avoiding health hazards, and to first-aid responses if things go wrong.

Chemicals in the eyes
Both resins and resin additives can damage the eyes; in the case of **peroxide**-based additives, they can cause permanent blindness by attacking the optic nerve. As result, it is *essential* that safety goggles be worn at all times when handling them, and that you have a professional eyewash station in an easy-to-reach place in your studio. The chemical name of the resin and additive you use (e.g. methyl ethyl ketone peroxide 33% strength) should be written down and kept near this station. If you are unlucky enough to get resin or resin additive in your eyes, this will help doctors to treat you properly once you get to hospital. Should you get a peroxide-

based additive in your eyes, you should rinse them with eyewash for a minimum of 30 minutes and then go straight to the casualty department of a specialist eye hospital.

Chemicals on the skin

Peroxide additives are extremely strong bleaches and will burn you. For this reason, they should be handled wearing anti-corrosive gloves and aprons or overalls. Should you get additives on your skin, wash them off immediately with warm water. If you are burned, seek medical help.

Inhaling chemicals

Most polyester resins contain a chemical called **styrene** which has been proven to be carcinogenic (i.e. cancer-causing) when used over time. As well as this, long-term inhalation of chemical solvents will damage your brain and central nervous system. As a result, you should only ever handle glass resins in a well-ventilated space and wearing a chemical cartridge respirator. If at all possible, you should consider investing in a proper extraction system in your studio.

Swallowing chemicals

Treatment will depend on the chemical involved. In the case of peroxides, for example, you should drink large quantities of milk and induce vomiting; by contrast, doing either of those things if you have swallowed a polyester-based resin will only make the damage worse. Most adhesion-promoters contain **esters**, which are highly poisonous: as little as 10 ml can cause permanent blindness and irreversible damage to your liver, kidneys and heart; 60 ml will kill you.

Make sure you know the name of all the chemicals you use and their particular first-aid treatments. Remember, symptoms of poisoning by chemicals such as esters can take up to 48 hours to show. *Always* go to a doctor should you swallow any of them.

Fire

Resins and resin additives contain volatile chemicals and should always be stored in an airtight space which is kept at a more or less constant temperature, out of direct sunlight and away from sources of heat (i.e. radiators, glass kilns). Styrene in some resins has a flash-point of 31°C, which means that it can catch fire spontaneously at this temperature. It goes without saying that you should never smoke in your studio at any time.

If you do have a fire, it is important to know how to deal with it: spraying water on some chemical fires can make them explode. Always read the manufacturers' manuals that come with your particular resins and additives and have the correct kind of fire-extinguisher – usually foam or carbon dioxide (CO_2) – to hand to deal with them. The good news is that storing your chemicals carefully will lessen the health risks of long-term exposure to them and will also increase their shelf lives.

Spillages and leftovers

If you spill resin, cover it with sand or vermiculite and leave it. Once all the resin is absorbed, sweep up the sand or vermiculite and put it in an airtight storage container for disposal. Use the same container for any leftover resin. Pouring jugs, spatulas and open funnels can all be cleaned using a specialist cleaning agent provided by your resin suppliers. (Note that nonspecialist cleaners such as acetone can react dangerously with the chemicals in your resin and should not be used.) In practice, simply wiping jugs and other implements thoroughly with absorbent paper immediately after use works just as well as using a specialist cleaning agent. Liquid resin dries to produce a nontoxic waste.

Environmental issues

As you might imagine, laminating resins and additives need to be disposed of carefully. Pouring toxic chemicals down the drain is illegal in the UK and many other countries, as is putting them out for domestic rubbish collection. Do either of these things and you will face heavy fines. Your local authority will be able to provide you with advice on the safe and legal disposal of toxic waste.

The dangers of glass

It goes without saying that chemical resins are only one of the hazardous materials you will be working with as a glass laminator. The other, obviously, is glass itself. A broken glass artwork may spell financial disaster, but it is also potentially lethal. Always wear specialist glass-handling gloves when working with glass: even the most innocuous-looking piece of glass can have sharp edges or hidden cracks, and most glass artists have their own horror stories involving trips to hospital and buckets of blood. Make sure that your first-aid kit is kept fully stocked with bandages, plasters and butterfly sutures in case of accident, and that you know your blood group.

CHAPTER NINE

Working on a larger scale (1)

Although you will now have a better idea of the different kinds of things you can do with laminated glass, the truth is that the market for 500 mm x 500 mm panels is small. If you are reading this book, then the chances are that you are thinking of working on a larger scale: perhaps of making big pieces for hanging on walls, or maybe even of making pieces that actually *are* the walls, so-called 'architectural glass' pieces.

With the growth of glass as an archi-tectural component – most big civic and commercial buildings now effectively consist of a glass skin hung from a steel skeleton – so the demand for art-glass that plays a structural role in buildings has grown. This means that artists working in laminated glass are often called in on architectural projects at an early stage in the design process. Large glass pieces may also be built into an existing structure at a later stage.

This, in turn, means that artists need to be familiar with all kinds of non-artistic things: commissioning strategies, contracts, fixtures and fittings and public safety requirements. These will be con-sidered in the next chapter. First, making large-scale laminated glass artworks calls for a different way of working in the studio, and maybe some extra equip-ment, so we will now look at some of the issues involved.

Making larger pieces in the studio

You may need the following additional equipment to make larger pieces:

At least one padded work table
Large, strong boards covered in felt
  or carpet
Two pairs of glass suckers
Wooden (or padded metal) frails
Mechanical tilting table (optional)
Palette truck (optional)

Although most of the processes dis-cussed in this book remain the same whatever scale you are working on – mixing resins, health and safety issues and so on – working with a piece of glass that is 2500 mm x 2500 mm is obviously going to be different from working with a piece that is 500 mm x 500 mm. One thing that remains constant in glass is that it is immensely fragile: even so-called 'toughened' or tempered glasses can have their corners knocked off if they are handled badly in the studio.

So the first thing that you are going to need, obviously, is space. Glass, for the most part, does not bend. It does break, though, especially when it is hit against a wall while being moved around. The ideal glass studio will have enough space for glass to be moved without too much

Interior of Yorgos Studio

manoeuvring. The studio will also be on the ground floor – stairs and lifts are the natural enemies of sheet glass – and have a shutter door or other source of easy access for glass deliveries.

The second thing you will need is at least one horizontal surface large, flat, stable and padded enough to cope with your work. As we have already seen, freshly laminated panels need to be kept as flat as possible while they are curing. They also need to rest on a surface that will not scratch them while they are being worked on. For this reason, it is a good idea to make yourself (or, if you can afford to, have yourself made) at least one strong wooden table, adjusted and tested with a spirit level to see that it is absolutely flat and covered in thick felt or carpet. If you move this table, test it

with your spirit level again. The table itself may be flat, but the floor on which it is now sitting may not be.

The third thing you will need is a number of suitably-sized carpeted boards for storing panels upright against your studio walls, before they are used or after they are finished. Even better, you should either buy or make yourself a set of frails, A-profile wooden or padded metal frames on which glass sheets can be stored at an angle before or after use. If you lean a glass panel on a wall without support of this kind, it will begin to bend under its own weight. This will increase the chances of your glass breaking, or your finished panel delaminating. If possible, designate a 'quiet wall' in your studio where these panels can sit without being in the way. And also make

72

Space is critical for making larger pieces

sure you have lots of old carpet, cut to useful sizes, for resting panels on during storage and while they are being moved around the studio. Glass corners are especially vulnerable to damage.

Finally, always bear in mind the question of weight. Glass may be pretty and delicate, but it is also very, very heavy. A two-face laminated panel weighs around 45 kg per square metre: a 200 mm x 1000 mm piece will thus weigh over 90 kg, or rather more than the average glass artist.

If you are going to be working on this scale, then you will need at least one part-time assistant who is familiar with (for example) the use of glass suction pads, and who knows how to plug a leak at one end of your freshly-poured panel if you happen to be at the other end when the leak happens. Most failures in laminated glass artworks come about because panels have been moved badly, and this happens when you have too few hands doing the moving. In this regard, it will also be helpful if you have a mechanical tilting table and a palette truck, if you can afford them.

74

Working on a larger scale (2)

Making larger-scale artworks not only calls for changes in your studio practice, it also means that you will have to become familiar with the way the architectural glass market works: commissioning procedures, contract protocols, public safety standards for architectural glass and so on. This chapter looks at the main things you will have to take into account.

Commissions and how to find them

As a rule of thumb, the more portable your artwork, the easier it will be to market. Taking a sample 500 mm x 500 mm panel around galleries or art fairs is not much of a problem. The same cannot be said of a 2500 mm x 2500 mm panel.

Architectural glass needs to be commissioned; the difficult thing is finding the commissions. A good place for British artists to start is with the Crafts Council, which can point you towards schemes like the Percent for Art programme and other commissioning agencies. The Council can also help with setting-up, equipment and maintenance grants. Art-glass studios may also pass on commissions to artists they regard as being in their 'stable', so touring these studios with samples and a portfolio is another good thing to do.

Contracts and contractual liability

As another rule of thumb, the larger your artwork, the more likely it is that you will have to deal with contracts and questions of contractual liability. An art consultant who buys a small painting to hang on a public wall will not, by and large, worry about that painting degrading with time or falling off the wall and hurting someone. By contrast, an art consultant who commissions a large piece of laminated glass to be built *into* a public wall will worry about both of those things. Equally, the artist responsible for the small painting is not going to be overly bothered about questions of transportation, copyright or insurance, while the artist who made the hypothetical piece of architectural glass very probably will be.

To make sure that both sides in any large-scale glass commission are happy, you need to have a watertight contract. Again, professional bodies like artists' unions can help you write up a good, standard, pro forma contract which should cover most of your commissions. In the UK, the *Artists' Newsletter* website offers a variety of standard contracts to cover most artist-client variables. The following issues are likely to be of specific interest to artists working in laminated glass.

Exhibiting at relevant trade fairs is a way to expose your work

Shelf life guarantees

One thing that any client commissioning an expensive, large-scale laminated glass artwork is likely to demand is some assurance that the artwork in question will not suddenly degrade. The problem with laminated glass pieces is that it is very difficult to give such guarantees. While Pilkington plc can simulate 50 years' worth of exposure to sunlight and temperature change in its research and development centre, it is highly unlikely that you will be able to do the same in your studio. Glass-art lamination is in its

infancy, and remains experimental. If you take it up, you will be making artworks using materials and processes that are, for the most part, not really meant for creative use. While a double-glazing firm may be able to guarantee that the resins it uses to glue two panes of glass together will not go yellow, fade or unstick in the next 20 years, an artist who is dying those same resins or using them to laminate linen to spray-painted glass cannot.

As a result, you (and your client) have to be realistic about the kinds of guarantees you give for the shelf life of any artwork. Generally, it would be wise to refuse to give contractual shelf life guarantees of longer than 12 months.

National and international safety standards

One of the problems for any architect is the enormous premiums payable for public liability insurance (i.e. the insurance that covers architects if any part of their building injures a member of the public). If you make architectural glass pieces, or even free-standing works capable of causing injury (and this includes most glass artworks), then you will become part of the architect's problem too. Therefore, art commissioners are always called upon to prove that the glass artworks they put in public spaces satisfy the demands of national safety boards such as, in the UK, the British Standards Institution (BSI).

Again, while Pilkington plc can run its own Human Impact Resistance Test

OPPOSITE: 'White Grid' BA Lounge, Heathrow Terminal 4, Yorgos Studio (2001)

'Waves1', private residence, Yorgos Studio (2002)

'Rock Slice,' Berkeley Square House, Yorgos Studio (2003)

to make sure that its flat safety glass fulfils the BSI's BS 6206 performance requirements, you will not be able to do the same. As a result, you should not allow yourself to be pushed into claiming public safety specifications on behalf of your artworks that those artworks simply will not live up to in practice. If the client needs your work to be BSI-guaranteed fireproof, blast-proof or bulletproof, then it is up to the client to find a way of making sure that it is. This can be done relatively easily by sandwiching your work between bulletproof glass and then having it tested, but it is not up to you to do the testing, or to provide the end client with national safety assurances.

Delivery and installation

One of the great grey areas of large-scale glass commissions is the vexed question of who is responsible for the safe delivery and installation of the work. Wherever possible, you should make sure that the client takes contractual responsibility for your artwork from the moment it leaves your studio.

Specialist art movers usually have little or no experience of moving glass, while specialist glass movers have no experience of moving art. While the latter's insurance will cover them (and you) for the cost of raw materials should your piece be broken in transit, it will not cover you (or them) for the value of the piece as a work of art. Taking out your own insurance for work in transit will be prohibitively expensive. I have seen a large and unwieldy panel, worth thousands of pounds, loaded from my studio onto a van by a single man whose day job was the delivery of double-glazing units, and all because the client in question wanted to save himself a couple of hundred pounds in transportation costs. If the panel had broken, it would have been the client's fault, but it would still have meant that six months' worth of my hard work had been destroyed, which wouldn't have made me particularly happy.

The same applies to installing the work. *Always* make sure that you have pre-agreed the context and fittings that will be used to house your work, and that the installation will be done by a properly qualified operative. Good work can be ruined by bad display; even if it is somebody else's property, it is still an advertisement (good or bad) for you.

Keeping control

One of the problems with any site-specific work is that the nature of the site itself can change with time. Today's swanky restaurant is tomorrow's pizza parlour, or worse. The owners who originally bought your work may take their paintings with them when they go, but they may not be so keen on paying to have walls knocked down so as to remove built-in architectural glass panels.

Although you cannot stop your work from being sold on, left behind or ruined by redecoration, you can (and should) insert a legally binding clause in your contract that requires your original client to consult you before any of these things happen. If you do not like the new context in which your work will find itself, you can insist on having your signature – and anything else (such as labelling) that identifies it as having been made by you – removed from it.

ALEXANDER BELESCHENKO

In order to gain an idea of how important it is to keep contractual control of your work after it has left your studio, consider the case of the well-known glass artist Alexander Beleschenko. In the summer of 2002, Beleschenko was passing through Reading railway station when he noticed that something was missing: namely one of his own artworks, a 40-ft-high tower of laminated glass that had been commissioned by British Rail back in 1989 and had dominated the station's passenger concourse for more than a decade. After the Reading line was taken over by First Great Western, a survey suggested that Beleschenko's work might not satisfy the latest BSI requirements. As a result, the piece was quietly removed in 1999. When asked where it had been stored, a railway spokesman nervously replied, 'Probably in a skip'. Beleschenko was understandably furious, and not just because it would have been a relatively easy

matter to test the piece and strengthen it if necessary. The German Glass Museum in Linnisch had

shown an interest in acquiring the work, and it had been valued at £60,000.

40-ft-high tower of laminated glass, Reading. Alexander Beleschenko, 1992, © Crafts Council Photostore

A Hertfordshire case study

If you are considering working in laminated glass, then it is likely that you will sooner or later find yourself taking on a commission that will require you to work with architects, art consultants, interior designers, builders or any permutation of the four. As well as learning a whole new way of working in the studio, you may well have to learn other things as well: how to publicise your work, how to win commissions, how to negotiate and write contracts, and how to transport, insure and install your finished pieces, to name but a few. So I thought it would be useful if I took you through one of my own recent projects, from beginning to end.

The commission in question was to make a four-panel, double-height opaque glass installation for the head of a staircase in a new house in Hertfordshire, designed by a well-known firm of London architects. Establishing a good relationship with your clients is one of the keys to producing good work, so it is as well to set off on a professional footing right from the start.

In September 2000, I showed at a London trade fair called 100% Design, part-funded by a Crafts Council bursary. This particular fair – which brings together artists, architects, designers and potential clients – has always been a good place for me to show. However, as is the way with these things, my Hertfordshire commission had nothing to do with 100% Design. In fact, my would-be clients had seen my degree-show work hanging in a London restaurant, and had asked their architects to contact me directly, which they did in early 2001.

The concept and the contract

At my first meeting, the architects explained the two main concepts behind the design of the new house: that it should blur the lines between 'inside' and 'outside'; and that it should be used to showcase the work of five chosen artists. Being brought in on a project at such an early stage is immensely useful, since it means that the various creative teams are working with, rather than against, each other. When I visited the site soon after this first meeting, I immediately saw where my own inspiration would come from: namely, in bringing a mature weeping beech tree in the garden into the new house, while at the same time excluding the ugly back wall of a house on the adjoining property. Glass is particularly good for playing around with inclusion and exclusion in this way, and I set about producing my presentation for my first meeting with the clients.

outside inside bringing the outside **inside**

opening framing images opening framing

Visiting the site

Finding a concept

You should go along to your first client meeting armed with two things: obviously, a good portfolio of your work so that the clients can see the kind of art you make; but also with some idea in your mind of what their project is going to cost them. Most clients are going to look for a rationale to your costing, and in my case it was based on the price of an earlier, single panel that I had sold to British Airways. The logic of this appealed to the client, as did my design ideas. So we agreed that I would issue a contract, with all further contractual details to be handled by the architects.

My standard contract is based on a template that can be downloaded for free from the website of the *Artists' Newsletter*, and can be altered according to the variables of each commission. In

OPPOSITE: Drawings for conceptual presentation

the case of the Hertfordshire house, the clients agreed to a three-part contract. The first part described a preliminary design stage, where I would be paid a fee to produce concept sketches along with the four other artists. The second part listed another fee to make a sample panel of the final work. The third part required me to produce the finished work to a precise deadline, with half of the main fee to be paid up front (to cover the cost of materials and other expenses) and the remaining half on completion.

It should be stressed here that a standard, three-part contract like this generally allows clients to bale out during the first and second stages if they

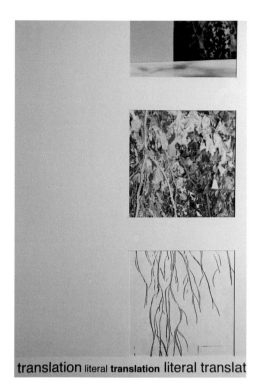

translation literal **translation** literal translat

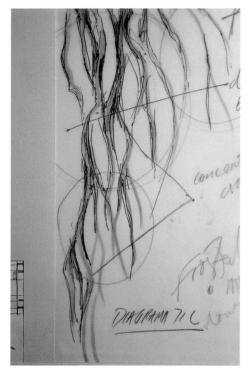

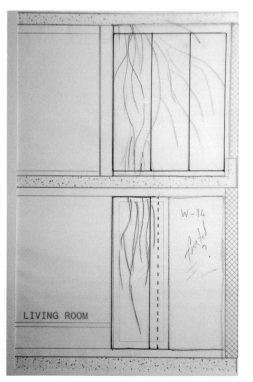

LIVING ROOM

A model to scale

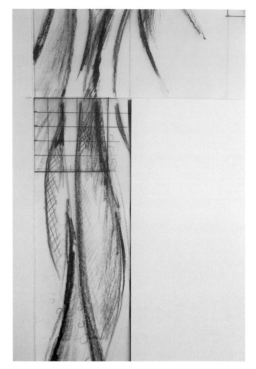

Drawing for final design presentation

do not like what they see, so it is as well to make sure that your initial presentations are done as slickly as they can possibly be. I took a lot of trouble over my first presentation, producing not just concept drawings but a small-scale maquette of the finished house, with a miniature model of my work *in situ*. The architects and clients were duly impressed.

Making the work

In the case of this particular work, 'Willow', I decided that I wanted the cracks in my pre-cracked laminated glass 'canvas' to read as abstract branches, with leaves to be implied by surface-applied pigments. I also wanted large areas of the finished glass to be more or

less opaque, so I sandblasted it using the sandblaster I had bought with the help of a Crafts Council setting-up grant.

Having done this, my first move was to mask each sheet of glass all the way around its perimeter with a 5 mm deep edge of masking tape. (This would keep pigments away from the edges where the double-sided adhesive tape would later be applied.) Once this was done, I diluted polyester paste pigments with methylated spirits until they were thin enough to seep into the cracks in my glass. Then I poured these pigments onto the cracks and waited for them to seep in (or 'travel') until I liked the way they looked. When they had done this, I wiped off any excess pigments with a meths-soaked cloth until the glass surface was absolutely clean.

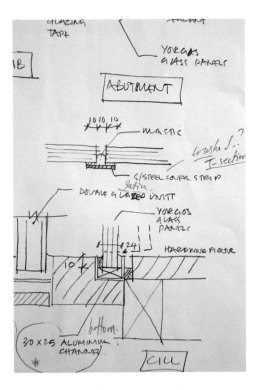

Architect's detailed drawing of fixings

Sample of the work to scale, for final design presentation

In a multi-panel commission like this, it is *vital* to work out a strict regime for applying your pigments. Renaissance fresco-painters, using pigments that dried quickly, worked in *giornatti* or 'day-patches', where all areas of a single colour were applied on the same day (because of the difficulty of getting exactly the same mix of colour two days running). In the same way, I worked on all four of my panels at the same time, applying the blacks one day, greens the next and so on. You should always make sure that your studio has enough table-space to allow for this.

When I had finished working with the liquid pigments, I went over the areas of glass I wanted to stay opaque once my resin was poured and treated them with a sand-sealing agent. (Resin, being liquid, tends to fill in the irregularities in a sandblasted glass surface and turn it transparent again. If you want specific areas of a sandblasted panel to stay opaque, then you have to seal them with a special sealant.) When this was done, I began to play around with my surface paints, this time using undiluted poly-ester paste pigments and applying them with brushes, cloths and gloved fingers. Once the decoration of the panels was finished, I started to laminate them: the three panels for the upstairs area in one-face laminate (since they would be too high up for anyone to see their obverse sides), and the more visible lower panel in two-face. As you would imagine, this did not happen overnight. From the moment I ordered my first glass sheets to when my

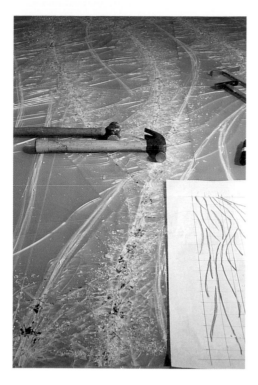

finished panels were finally lifted off their laying tables took around six months of more or less constant work.

Storage and installation

Although architects worry about glass artists being able to meet legal public safety requirements, artists working in glass also need to worry about architects meeting deadlines. In the case of this particular project, completion of the Hertfordshire house overran by almost a year. This could have landed me in a lot of trouble. One thing you must *always* make sure of in your contract is that you are covered for any delay, i.e. that the clients or their agents agree to remove your work from your studio as soon as it is finished, and to store it and insure it at their own expense

Breaking the glass along the design

BELOW: Applying diluted pigment into cracks

ABOVE: Working on the panel after the application of sandseal *BELOW:* *LEFT,* Inserting boning sticks and funnel in preparation for laminating *RIGHT,* Pouring the resin (an envelope pour)

LEFT: Checking that the work is level

until they are ready to install it. If this had not been stipulated in my contract, I could have been left with four large glass panels, weighing a total of 250 kg and valued in the tens of thousands of pounds, cluttering up my studio for the best part of a year. Insuring these would have been unaffordably expensive, and yet I could not have afforded not to: in the small studio I then had, the risk of breakage would have been too high. More importantly, if I had to keep the finished panels in my studio, there simply would not have been any room left for me to work in. Storing the panels for a year myself could easily have put me out of business.

BELOW, LEFT AND RIGHT: Installation of 'Willow' OPPOSITE Hertfordshire work in situ

90

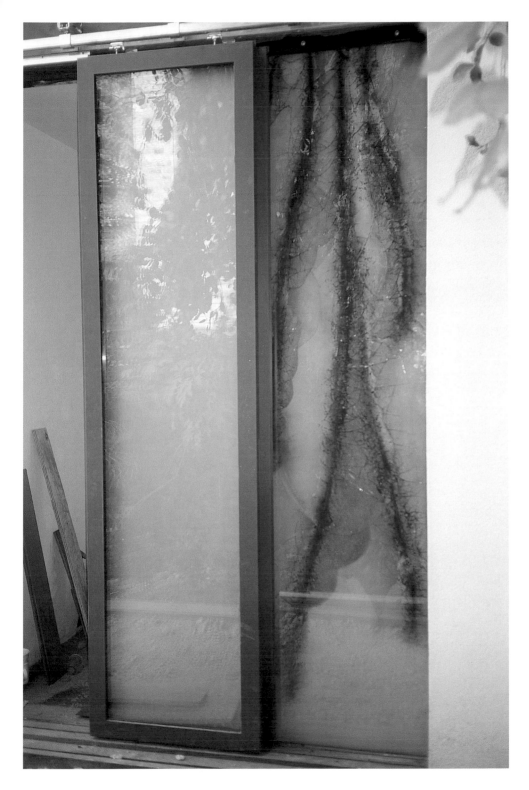

Hertfordshire work in situ

You should always make sure that you are included in any decisions about the installation of your work. Bad display can ruin the effect of a piece, and bad handling can damage it. In the case of this project, I pre-agreed the framing and fittings with the architects: we used aluminium channels for the invisible top, bottom and side supports, and more expensive brushed stainless steel strips to define the visible joins between the various panels. All the panels would be backlit by natural light during the day, and by an external flat light source at night. I also made sure that I was on site during the actual installation, to make sure that (for example) the back of each panel was completely clean before it was fixed, irremovably, into a wall.

It sounds an obvious thing to say, but working in architectural glass requires you to think about dozens of different things at once: not just aesthetic concerns, but practical, legal and commercial ones. The Hertfordshire project was a success in aesthetic terms, and also because it went so well on all levels. Both clients and architects remain keen supporters of my studio as a result.

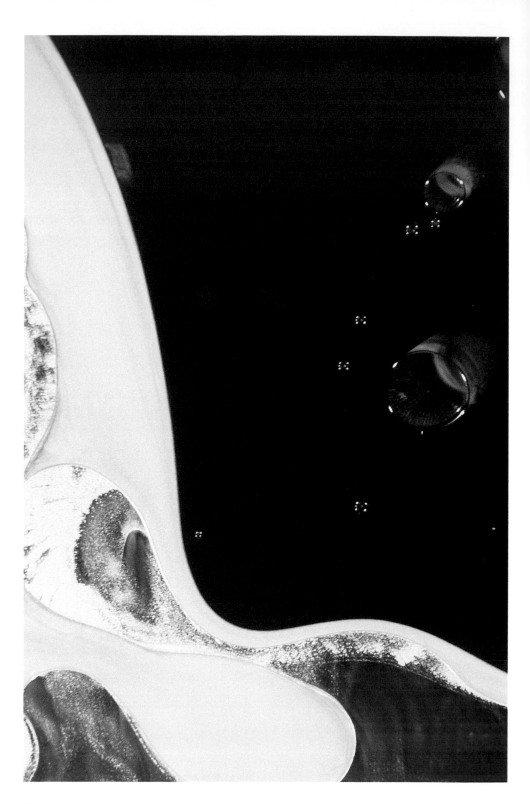

CHAPTER TWELVE

Problems and how to solve them

It cannot be repeated often enough that making artworks out of laminated glass is a tricky thing to do. Most glass resins – and most float glasses, come to that – are manufactured with an industrial or semi-industrial end in mind. This means that most resin producers and glassmakers do not really expect their products to be used in the inventive way in which you will probably want to use them.

What these manufacturers see, in their commercial minds' eye, is flat glass being laminated to flat glass for a good practical reason, for example, sound insulation, impact-resistance or fireproofing. What they *don't* see is using resins to laminate shattered glass onto (or between) sheets of plain glass. Resins are not really designed to seep into cracks or bullet-holes in an artistic way, or to react well with pastels or inks or pieces of metal that happen to have caught an artist's eye. These resin manufacturers also assume that you will have expensive industrial equipment to apply them with under controlled conditions, and that there will be a team of trained operatives to help you as you do so.

Since neither of these things is likely to apply to you as an artist, you will have to come to terms with the fact that much of what you do is going to be the outcome of trial and error. This makes glass lamination an exciting medium to

work in: many of your favourite pieces may come about, at least in part, as the result of accidents. But it must also be said that accidents are very much less appealing when they happen in the middle of a £10,000 commission, or the day before you are due to deliver a large architectural panel to an art consultant. So the following section looks at the most common problems you may have to face, what lies behind those problems and the most effective ways of dealing with them.

Problems during pouring

You spot a foreign body in the resin

This can happen if you have been careless with cleaning your equipment, or if you have forgotten to sieve your resin and/or cover it once it is mixed. Always keep a clean piece of glass rod to hand during pouring, and use this to fish out any foreign object you might spot. Once dust or a hair is in the glass, it is too late to do anything about it.

Resin leaks from your glass envelope

This can happen if you have either been careless about storing your adhesive tape (moisture causes it to lose its stickiness) or about making sure your glass is absolutely clean. If your panel starts to leak liquid resin as you are pouring, it is because the tape has not bonded properly to the glass. Mop up as much resin as you can using disposable cloth or paper and put it in your airtight waste area: it will set into a nontoxic plastic. Prise your panels apart carefully, dry them thoroughly, clean them and start all over again.

The resin starts to set as you pour

This time, you have miscalculated one or more of the following: the amount of additive you need; the time you have left your resin to stand; or the temperature at which you are working. (Generally speaking, the hotter it is, the quicker your resin will set.) If your piece is sufficiently robust, i.e. relatively plain, you can split your laminate carefully after four to five hours, scrape the dried resin off with a blade, wipe away any sediment with meths and start all over again. Needless to say, the chances of breakage are high. If your laminate involves separate pieces, shattered glass, fabrics, wood or other non-glass materials, then you might as well throw it away.

Problems after pouring

The resin does not set in the prescribed time

This will be obvious to the naked eye: the liquid resin will ooze around under the glass if you press or move it. Chances are that you have miscalculated the amount of additive you need to set the resin. If the glass is expensive, carefully drill a hole in the adhesive tape/silicone gel perimeter and drain the resin away; split the laminate carefully and start again.

Air bubbles or pockets in the resin

This can happen for all kinds of reasons, although the most common is that your laminated panel has not been laid flat. Check the surface of your glass with a spirit level and, if the resin has not set, adjust it accordingly. If flatness does not seem to be the problem, then you either have not sealed your edges properly (this is especially likely if the bubble or pocket is near the edge of the panel) or you have not used enough resin. This is a particular problem if you have been laminating uneven, non-glass materials like wood, absorbent materials like cloth, or shattered glass sheets: increased internal surface area requires increased resin, although no manufacturer's instructions can tell you exactly how much. It is best to include 20–25% more resin than recommended when making shattered glass pieces.

If air bubbles are small they can be attractive; depending on the work, I tend to leave them alone. They are also stable and will not grow or change with time. If they are large or look bad, you can insert a syringe through the siliconed edge of your work and inject fresh resin into the air pocket, provided the initial resin has not fully set. However, the needle you use will leave a track-mark in part-set resin, so make sure you really cannot live with the air bubbles before you do this.

A fern-shaped air pocket appears

Air bubbles or pockets look like what they are, i.e. they have even edges and are round or oblong. They are also spottable from the moment you have finished laminating. If an uneven pocket begins to appear, then you're facing something much, much nastier: namely **delamination**, the bane of any glass laminator's life.

Manufacturers' manuals tend to suggest that delamination takes place because you have not poured enough resin into your laminate. But it may be that you have moved the piece too soon after laminating, or that excessive force has been used in moving it. (This is especially likely if you have used glass suckers to move a large panel.) It may be that you have used stale or incorrectly mixed resin, or that you have not cleaned your glass, or that there has been a violent change of temperature in your studio during setting, or that you are just having an incredibly bad day. Sometimes there is no other explanation.

Whatever the cause, there is nothing to be done. There is no cure for delamination, and once it has started it can go on spreading, quickly or slowly. It can occur within hours of pouring resin, and can appear, suddenly and inexplicably, in works that have been sitting about quite happily for days or even weeks or months. Just accept it as philosophically as you can, and try to keep your client calm.

The resin interlayer cracks

This comes about when you add too much curing additive to your resin. As with delamination, it will continue to spread until the entire work is affected. As with delamination, there is nothing to be done.

The resin interlayer goes milky

You have got water in your resin, usually as a result of poor storage practice. There is no cure.

Conclusion

During the course of writing this book, I have been surprised to discover how much is going on in the world of art lamination. When you spend most of your time bent over a sheet of glass, it is easy to lose sight of the bigger picture. Massive, minimalist architectural pieces are being made in New York for shipment to Hong Kong; small, wacky works are being made in Germany for the windows of local churches; laminated glass installations can be found in everything from private country houses to urban metro stations. What links all these very dissimilar artworks is their sense of excitement; and this has much to do with working in a medium that is industrial, and whose use in the fine arts is still largely experimental.

As a result, the other thing I have learned is how much there still is to learn. Finding out how other artists are using laminates has made me stand back and consider my own practice. It has also made me keen to try out new materials: glass with photovoltaic cells built into it, resins that change colour with light. Artists are often shy of sharing their discoveries for fear of being copied, but those of us working with laminated glass need (like our panels) to stick together.

GLOSSARY

Acid etching: a process in which hydrofluoric acid is worked into the surface of glass to produce patterns. Different resists can be used to mask out specific areas for decorative etching. It is an extremely dangerous process and safety precautions are mandatory.

Autoclave: a large industrial pressure-cooker in which heat and pressure are applied in a controlled environment to bond two or more sheets of glass together with PVB interlayer. Autoclaves are used for the production of laminated glass in industry.

Boning sticks: plastic spatulas used to separate two sheet of glass during resin pouring.

BS 6206: performance requirements demanded by the British Standards Authority for flat glass used in building.

Cast in place (CIP): a process in which glass is laminated by hand, by pouring liquid resin into the space between two or more sealed sheets.

Celluloid: a plastic made from camphor and nitrocellulose.

Craquelure: the network of small cracks in a pigment, glaze or varnish.

Crystal glass: glass made with lead oxide as a major flux.

Dammed area: the area on a glass sheet marked out with a 'dam' of adhesive tape, to be filled in with liquid resin.

Delamination: term used to describe the 'unsticking' of a resin interlayer, usually as a result of poor studio practice or faulty resin. Delamination typically begins with the appearance of a 'fern pattern' air space between sheets of laminate, and can spread until the entire interlayer is involved.

Edging tape: a double-sided adhesive tape used around the edges of glass to build up a cavity into which resin will spread. It comes in a clear or foam form and in different thicknesses.

Enamels: the various coloured substances used to paint or print onto glass.

Envelope pour: process in which liquid resin is introduced to the space between two or more sheets of glass, sealed at the edges to form an 'envelope'.

Epoxy resin: a synthetic resin produced by co-polymerising epoxide compounds with phenols.

Ester: organic compound in which a hydrogen atom in an acid is replaced by an alkali.

Fern-shaped air pockets: a fern-shaped pattern occurring if two sheets of glass do not adhere well (see delamination). It can creep and spread until the two sheets separate entirely.

Float glass: the most commonly available sheet glass, made by floating liquid glass on molten tin.

Fusing: melting different layers of glass together in a kiln at temperatures of around 800°C.

Human Impact Resistance Test: a safety test carried out by industrial manufacturers in which a bag of lead shot is swung at a laminated sheet to test its resistance to the impact of a human body.

Kiln texturing: a process in which glass is textured by melting (or 'slumping') it over a mould in a heated glass kiln.

Kiln-formed glass/kiln forming: glass slumped or fused in a glass kiln.

Laminated glass: two or more sheets of glass bonded together. Also called safety glass. It is resistant to shattering and difficult to cut.

Lead glass: glass made with lead oxide as a major flux, also know as crystal glass.

Open funnel: a flat, stainless steel funnel used to introduce liquid resin into the space between sheets of glass in an envelope pour.

Polyester resin: resin that consists of styrene as its main ingredient.

Polyvinyl butyral (PVB): the plastic interlayer used in industry to laminate glass.

Resin: any viscous substance containing organic polymers and terpenoids, and which can be made to harden into a rigid bond.

Resist: a material used to cover areas of glass to mask them from the effect of acid etching or sandblasting.

Safety glass: a loose term, used to describe a wide variety of glasses that have been strengthened to resist shattering. Tempered, toughened, laminated and wired glasses are included in this category.

Sandblasting: a process in which abrasive materials (sand or grit) are forced against a glass surface under pressure, usually from compressed air.

Sandseal: a sealant used to coat the sandblasted areas of a glass sheet before it is laminated with resin, to preserve the effect of sandblasting.

Shattered laminate: term used to describe a triple laminate in which the middle layer is a sheet of toughened glass that has been shattered after lamination between two sheets of float glass.

Soda-lime glass: glass with a high sodium oxide content. The most commonly available sheet glass.

Stained glass: pieces of glass, usually coloured or painted and held in place by lead strips to produce decorative panels.

Suction pads: rubber pads that use a suction force to lift or manoeuvre glass.

Toughened (or tempered) glass: glass that has been rapidly heated and cooled in order to strengthen it.

Two-face laminate: a three-part panel that has been laminated on both sides.

Vermiculite: hydrous silicates made from decomposed mica. It is a very light compound, used as an insulating material and to absorb spillages.

DIRECTORY

Suppliers/manufacturers

Pollard Glass Transportation
53 Barnoldswick Road
Nelson
Lancashire BB9 6AT
Tel: +44 (0)1282 606125
Fax: +44 (0)1282 605150
E-mail: glassmovers@aol.com

Llewellyn Ryland Ltd (polyester colour pastes)
Haden High Street
Birmingham B12 9DB
Tel: +44 (0)121 440 2284
Fax: +44 (0)121 440 0281

Solutia Inc (PVB manufacturers)
Galaxy 219
6 bis, Rue de la Paroisse
78000 Versailles
France
Tel: +33 (0)1 30 83 90 26
Fax: +33 (0)1 30 83 90 27
E-mail: info@solutia.com
www.solutia.com

Prefit (architectural glass fittings)
14 Sovereign Park
Coronation Road
London NW10 7QP
Tel: +44 (0)20 8961 4777
Fax: +44 (0)20 8961 4747
E-mail: sales@prefitfittings.co.uk
www.prefit-fittings.com

Du Pont (PVB manufacturers)
Maylands Avenue
Hemel Hempstead

Herts HP2 7DP
Tel: +44 (0)1442 218 541
Fax: +44 (0)1442 218 663
www.dupont.com

Unilam International Ltd (resin suppliers)
Ravenscliffe Road
Leeds
West Yorkshire LS28 5RZ
Tel: +44 (0)1274 615 550
Fax: +44 (0)1274 615 540
E-mail: sales@unilaminternational.com
www.unilaminternational.com

Zircon Corporation (resin manufacturers)
PO Box 1270
Collierville
TN 38027-1270
USA
Tel: +1 901 853 4707
Fax: +1 901 853 8931
E-mail: cebayha@aol.com
www.zirconcorp.com

Uvelok (UV bonding)
Allée de la Recherche 60
1070 Brussels
Belgium
Tel: +32 (2)559 9999
Fax: +32 (2)559 9900
E-mail: uvelok@ucb-group.com
www.chemicals.ucb-group.com

Glasslam Europe Ltd (resin manufacturers)
Unit M1 Tribune Drive
Trinity Estate

Sittingbourne
Kent ME10 2PG
Tel: +44 (0)1795 423314
Fax; +44 (0)1795 430228
E-mail: glasslam@aol.com
www.glasslam.com

Glasslam NGI Inc.
(resin manufacturers)
2059 Blount Road
Pompano Beach
FL 33069
USA
Tel: +1 954 975 3233
Fax: +1 954 975 3225
E-mail: glasslam@icanect.net
www.glasslam.com

Surlyt (resin manufacturers)
5 The Cross
Dalry KA24 5AL
Tel: +44 (0)1294 832322
Fax: +44 (0)1294 832101
E-mail: surlyt@cqm.co.uk
www.1stlam.com

John Bell & Croyden (surgical and
medical suppliers)
50 – 54 Wigmore Street
London W1U 2AU
Tel: 0800 085 9012

Andrew Moor Associates (architectural
glass consultant)
14 Chamberlain Street
London NW1 8XB
Tel: +44 (0)20 7586 8181
E-mail: andrew@andrewmoor.co.uk
www.andrewmoor.co.uk

Glass studios

Yorgos Studio Ltd.
31 Tower Gardens Road
London N17 7PS
Tel: +44 (0)20 8885 2029
Fax: +44 (0)20 8885 1321
E-mail: info@yorgosglass.com
www.yorgosglass.com

Derix Glass Studios
D-65232 Taunusstein
Platterstrasse 94
Germany
Tel: +49 06128 96680
Fax: +49 06128 96686
E-mail: studio@derix.com
www.derix.com

Derix Art Glass Consultants
Oakland
CA USA
Tel: +1 510 268 1440
E-mail: derixcom@msn.com
www.derix.com

Creative Glass Studios
Tel: +44 (0)117 973 7025
E-mail: mike@creative-glass.co.uk
www.creative-glass.co.uk

Fusion Glass Designs Ltd
365 Clapham Road
London SW9 9BT
Tel: +44 (0)20 7738 5888
Fax: +44 (0)20 7738 4888

Joel Berman Glass Studios Ltd
Canada
Tel: +800 505 45277
www.jbermanglass.com

Ozone Glass Limited
Unit 1 Home Farm Business Centre
Home Farm Road, Brighton
East Sussex BN1 9HU
Tel: +44 (0)20 7351 0066
Fax: +44 (0)20 7351 0088
E-mail: info@ozoneglass.co.uk
www.ozoneglass.co.uk

Igloo
Garreg Wen Farmhouse
Borth Y Best
Porthmadog
Gwynedd LL49 9UG
Tel: +44 (0)1766 512 652
Fax: +44 (0)1766 514 852
E-mail: paulthom@beeb.net
www.igloo.uk.com

Glass suppliers/processors

Pilkington
Prescot Road
St Helens WA10 3TT
Tel: +44 (0)1744 692 000
Fax: +44 (0)1744 613 049
www.pilkington.co.uk

Rankings Glass
TWIdes
Glass House Field
London E1 9JA
Tel: +44 (0)20 7790 2333

Armfield Glass
191 Church Road
Benfleet
Essex SS7 4PN
Tel: +44 (0)1268 793067

Firmans Glass
19 Bates Road
Romford

Essex RM3 OJH
Tel: +44 (0)1708 374 534

Organisations

Laminated Glass Information Centre
(LGIC)
299 Oxford Street
London W1C 2DZ
Tel: +44 (0)20 7499 1720
Fax:+44 (0)20 7495 1106

National Glass Association
National Glass Centre
Liberty Way
Sunderland SR6 OGL
Tel: +44 (0)191 515 2031
Fax: +44 (0)191 515 2103
E-mail: info@nationalglasscentre.com

Society of Glass Technology
20 Hallam Gate Road
Sheffield S10 5BT
Tel: +44 (0)114 266 3168
Fax: +44 (0)114 266 5252
E-mail: gt@glass.demon.co.uk
www.glass.demon.co.uk

Glass Art Society Inc.
PO Box 1364
Corning
NY 14830
USA
Tel: +1 607 936 0530

Crafts Council
44a Pentonville Road
London N1 9BY
Tel: +44 (0)20 7278 7700

Artists referred to in this book

Christine Harfleet
56 Rodmell Ave
Brighton
Sussex BN2 8PG
Tel: +44 (0)1273 309666
chrissyharfleet@hotmail.com

Michele Oberdieck Textile Design
Unit 1.04 Oxo Tower Wharf
Barge House Street
London SE1 9PH
Tel: +44 (0)20 7261 1414
Fax: +44 (0)20 7261 1414
www.micheleoberdieck.co.uk

Hella Santarossa
Tel: +49 30 881 9562

James Carpenter Design Associates
145 Hudson Street
New York
NY 10013
USA
Tel: +1 212 431 4318
Fax: +1 212 431 4425
E-mail: info@jcdainc.com
www.jcdainc.com

Academic institutions

The following is a selected list of colleges
and universities offering glass courses:

Sunderland University
Backhouse Park
Ryhope Road
Sunderland
Tyne and Wear
Tel: +44 (0)191 515 2112
Fax: +44 (0)191 515 2132
www.sunderland.ac.uk

Swansea Institute of Higher Education
Mount Pleasant
Swansea SA1 6ED
Tel: +44 (0)1792 481 000
Fax: +44 (0)1792 481 085
E-mail: enquiry@sihe.ac.uk
www.sihe.co.uk

Royal College of Art
Ceramics & Glass Department
Kensington Gore
London SW7 2EU
tel: +44 (0)20 7590 4444
www.rca.ac.uk

London Institute
Central St Martins
Southampton Row
London WC1
Tel: +44(0)20 7514 7000

Wolverhampton University
Glass Dept.
Molineux Street
Wolverhampton WV1 1SB
Tel: +44(0)191 515 2000
www.wlv.ac.uk

Edinburgh College of Art
Lauriston Place
Edinburgh
Tel: +44(0)131 229 9311
www.eca.ac.uk

Sydney College of the Arts
The University of Sydney
Rozelle
NSW 20339
Australia
Tel: +612 9351 4079
Fax: +612 9351 4013
E-mail: info@usyd.edu.au
www.usyd.edu.au

Canberra School of Art
The ANU School of Art
GPO Box 804
Canberra ACT 2601
Australia
E-mail: csa.reception@anu.edu.au
www.anu.edu.au

Royal Melbourne Institute of Technology
Latrobe Street
Melbourne VIC 3000
Australia

Pilchuck Glass School
107 South Main Street
Seattle
WA 98104
USA
www.pilchuck.com

Bucks County Community College
275 Swamps Road
Newtown
PA 18940
USA
Tel: +1 215 968 8000
E-mail: webmaster@bucks.edu
www.bucks.edu

Staatliche Glasfachschule Rheinbach
Zentrum fur Glass-Keramik-Grafik
Zu den Fichten 19
D53359 Rheinbach
Germany
Tel: +49 2226 4425

The Gerrit Rietveld Academie
Frederick Roeskestraat 96
Amsterdam
The Netherlands

Additional websites

www.aecportico.co.uk
(laminated glass information centre)

www.corning.com
(glass technology-led products)

www.glass1usa.com
www.gulfglass.com
www.calglassbending.com
(glass bending)
www.glassbending.co.uk
(curved glass)

www.saflex.com
(laminated glass)

www.usglassmag.com
(*American Glass Magazine*)

www.creative-glass.co.uk
www.glassonweb.com
(flat-glass guide)

www.worldofglass.com
(glass centre at St Helens)

www.sgt.org
(Society of Glass Technology)

www.iop.co.uk
(Institute of Packaging)

www.glasspages.com
(directory of glass companies)

www.stainedglass.org
(Stained Glass Association of America)

www.glass.org
(National Glass Association)

www.britglass.co.uk
(British Glass Manufacturers
Confederation)

www.glassassociation.org.uk
www.pirelli.com
(fibre optics)

www.accu-glass.com
(glass tubing)

www.lambertglass.com
(mouthblown sheet glass)
www.saint-gobain-glass.com
(glass and glazing products)

www.bibby-sterilin.co.uk
(borosilicate glassware)

www.schott.com
(leading company in glass technology)

www.a-n.co.uk
(*Artists' Newsletter Magazine*)

Journals / periodicals

Glass
(Journal of the European Glass Industry)
International Publications
2 Queensway
Redhill
Surrey RH1 1QS

Glass Cone
(Journal of the Glass Association)
Broadfield House Glass Museum
Barnett Lane
Kingswinford
West Midlands DY6 9QA

Networks: Contemporary Glass Society Bulletin
The Surrey Institute for Art and Design
Farnham
Surrey

Neues Glas
Verlagsgesellschaft Ritterbach GmbH
PO Box 1820
D-50208 Frechen
Germany

Glass Age
Miller Freman
Sovereign Way
Tonbridge
Kent TN9 1RW

BIBLIOGRAPHY

This bibliography is intended as a guide to further reading, as well as an indication of sources used for this book.

Glass

Glass in Architecture and Decoration, Raymond McGrath, Architectural Press, London, 1961

Living Under Glass, Jane and Stafford Cliff, Thames and Hudson, London, 1986

The Art of Glass, Stephen Knapp, Rockport Publishers, Massachusetts, 1998

Contemporary Glass: A World Survey from the Corning Museum of Glass, Susanne K Frantz, Harry N Abrams Press, New York, 1989

Contemporary Art Glass, Ray and Lee Grover, Crown Publishers, New York, 1975

Architectural Glass Art, Andrew Moor, Mitchell Beazley, London,1997

Glass: A Contemporary Art, Dan Klein, Rizzoli, New York, 1989

An Illustrated Dictionary of Glass, Harold Newman, Thames and Hudson, London, 1977

Neues Glas in Europa / New Glass in Europe, Helmet Ricke, Verlanganstalt Handwerk, Dusseldorf, 1991

Glass: Its Traditions and its Makers, Ada Polak, G.P. Putnam's Sons, New York, 1975

Out of the Fire: Contemporary Glass Artists and Their Work, Bonnie Miller, Chronicle Books, San Fransisco, 1991

The History of Glass, Dan Klein and Ward Lloyd (eds), Orbis Publishing Ltd, 1984

Glass, Structure and Technology in Architecture, Sophia and Stefan Behlin (eds), Prestel Verlag, Munich, 1999

Designing with Glass, Carol Soucek King, PBC International Inc., New York, 1996

Dictionary of Glass Materials and Techniques, C Bray, A&C Black, London, 1995

Techniques of Kiln-formed Glass, Keith Cummings, A&C Black, London, 1997

The Beauty of Stained Glass, Patrick Reyntiens, London, 1990

Glass Materials for Inspirational Design, Chris Lefteri, Rotovision, Switzerland, 2002

Glass in Architecture, Michael Wigginton, Phaidon, London, 1996

Five Thousand Years of Glass, Hugh Tait, British Museum Press, London, 1991

Glass in Building, David Button and Brian Pye, Oxford, Butterworth Architecture, 1993

A History of Glass Making, RW Douglas and Susan Frank, GT Foulis and Co Ltd, 1972

Glass, Reino Liefkes, V&A Publications, London, 1997

Health and Safety

The Artist's Complete Health and Safety Guide, Monona Rossol, Allworth Press, New York 1990

Health Hazards Manual for Artists, Michael McCann, Nick Lyon Books, USA, 1985

INDEX